CRYSTALS

FOR

BEGINNERS

The Ultimate Beginners Guide to

Discover the Secret Power of

Crystals and Stones

CHRISTIE STONE

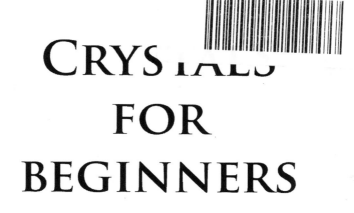

should be consulted as needed prior to undertaking any of the action endorsed herein.

This declaration is deemed fair and valid by both the American Bar Association and the Committee of Publishers Association and is legally binding throughout the United States.

Furthermore, the transmission, duplication or reproduction of any of the following work including specific information will be considered an illegal act irrespective of if it is done electronically or in print. This extends to creating a secondary or tertiary copy of the work or a recorded copy and is only allowed with an expressed written consent from the Publisher. All additional right reserved.

The information in the following pages is broadly considered to be a truthful and accurate account of facts, and as such any inattention, use or misuse of the information in question by the reader will render any resulting actions solely under their purview. There are no scenarios in which the publisher or the original author of this work can be in any fashion deemed liable for any hardship or damages that may befall them after undertaking information described herein.

Additionally, the information in the following pages is intended only for informational purposes and should thus be thought of as universal. As befitting its nature, it is presented without assurance regarding its prolonged validity or interim quality. Trademarks that are mentioned are done without written consent and can in no way be considered an endorsement from the trademark holder.

Table of Contents

Introduction

Ah, the crystals. These gorgeous gems have traditionally been used to help relieve stress and heal the body, and they make fab necklaces, bracelets and anklets as well. So it's no surprise that some folk, including rich and famous ones, have opted for crystal healing, a non-invasive therapy that relies on these sparkly, transparent gems for their perceived restorative and healthful properties.

Some people say it's all hype. But others - even well-known actors such as Shirley MacLaine and Michael York - say that crystals have unbelievable mystical powers that can heal and protect. They believe these cute little gems can do everything from protect people from muggers to help restore their dreams, and that they are more than a worthwhile investment.

The method is simple: Crystals or gemstones are places on parts of the body which are identified as "chakras," or having a specific life force. The body has seven main energy centers in and thus seven corresponding colors attached to them, so multi-colored crystals are employed.

The idea behind the crystals is that getting rid of all that nasty negative energy in a specific place can aid healing, which is what they are primarily used for. They get rid of the bad, and by doing so, heal and help bring in the good. Most crystal practitioners say that crystal healing is a way to focus yourself on what your body needs, much like a form of mediation. It is a complementary technique not intended to replace any type of medical care.

One way to look at it is like this: If you are battling a long-term illness with regular hospital care, crystal healing alongside your regular medication and therapies may help focus your optimism, give you a better sense of well-being and help you cope better. Or think of it this way: Investing money in little pieces of crystal is nothing but a complete waste of time, and a way for self-proclaimed crystal therapists to scam cash off innocent and naive (and also desperate) people.

Types of Crystal Healing

Most people believe crystal therapy works only by visiting a crystal practitioner. While this is the most well-known method, there are other applications which can have the same effect (or no effect at all!). They include:

- As mentioned, visit a crystal healer, or someone who is trained in the art of crystal healing. They can place specific crystals on you to heal a certain ailment.

- Wear a gemstone or crystal to keep you healthy, and heal and protect you as you go throughout your daily life.

- Place a crystal or several crystals in your bed. When you sleep you will feel recharged.

- Put crystals in your bathwater as you bathe for a wet, re-energizing experience.

- Use crystals during a specialized crystal meditation. This can be achieved either by holding a crystal or placing it next to you. Try and meditate while concentrating on the crystal powers.

- Use them in crystal reflexology and/or massage. Rub smooth crystals on your skin for maximum effect.

- Soak a crystal in water then drink it (with the crystal removed!). For something a bit more fun, make a crystal essence with a soaked crystal or gem, water and alcohol.

Crystal Clear Rules

Followers of crystal therapy believe you should follow these rules to get the most from your crystals:

- Always thoroughly cleanse a crystal before handling it. Remember they can hold another individual's energy, so this is important. How you cleanse them is irrelevant, you can use water, light, herbs or pure sound vibrations, if you wish.

- All good crystals need to recharge from time to time, so give them a break.

- Don't forget that when you acquire a new crystal you should always "program and dedicate" it, clearly stating your intention. Do this in advance of using it unless you want all its healing properties to be depleted.

- Like people, different crystals have different properties. Many people believe that crystals actually choose you because of what they can offer you. Is the decision you made the correct choice? Only you have the answer...

The Verdict is Crystal Clear

Like magnet therapy, crystal therapy is generally seen as a non-invasive type of alternative treatment that can have no adverse effects, and is therefore worth a try. That's true, as long as you don't forsake conventional medicine in favor of it, or shell out the entire contents of your wallet on a fancy crystal that just collects dust on your mantelpiece.

If you want to try crystal therapy, give it a go. But you must have an open - some would say extremely gullible - mind for it to work.

Crystal Healing

Energy and Protection

Everything in the physical world is made up of energy and information. Energy vibrates at different frequencies but we are unable to see this energy because it is vibrating too fast for us. Because our senses are too slow for these vibrations, we only receive chunks of information that allows us to perceive the chair we are sitting on, our body, other people and so on.

When you walk into a room and it feels like you can 'cut the atmosphere with a knife', this is referred to as negative energy and likewise, if you go to a party, you hopefully will feel excitement in the air - or positive energy.

In the same way, when we open up our energy centres in healing, meditation, prayer, visualisation or working with crystals, we are attracting energy vibrations to us (negative as well as positive). It is therefore necessary that we protect ourselves from the negative energy.

Grounding

Grounding is important to perform before you start to work with your crystals as it keeps you in touch with your earthly surroundings. Working with crystals will take you onto a higher plane and when you finish your work, if you have not grounded yourself beforehand, you may experience a floating feeling and be emotional (like a healing curve) as you have opened yourself up and could be susceptible to other's negativity.

To ground yourself, take three depth breaths, sitting with feet firmly on the ground and visualise that there are roots extending from the bottom of your feet. They are growing down through the floor, through the earth and right down through to the centre of the earth to ensure that you are fully grounded. To test your grounding, try to lift your foot from the floor. If you find this difficult, you know you have grounded yourself correctly.

Prayer

Dear Universe I ask that you surround me with the pure white light of your divine being. Remove me from all negative vibrations to be dispersed in the universe without harm to any living thing. Please place me in my own golden bubble of complete absolute protection.

Visualisation

Visualise yourself standing in a pink bubble and know that nothing can penetrate this bubble only divine white light and unconditional love.

White is the colour of divine protection and pink is the colour of unconditional spirit love.

Cleansing and Blessing your Crystals

There are many ways that crystals can be cleansed. However, not all crystals can be placed in water without being damaged so it is important that you are careful about the way you cleanse your crystals.

When crystals are obtained from Interactions all manual cleansing has been done. If your crystals were obtained elsewhere then you will have to cleanse them yourself.

With so much pollution and dust in atmosphere, it is advised that a baby's hairbrush is used to brush the crystals, which not only removes the dust but also gently stimulates the crystal at the same time.

Crystals also need to be blessed before use. Once the crystal has been manually cleansed the following prayer is required so that the crystal is ready to work with you.

A Blessing

Dear Universe I give thanks to mother earth for giving these crystals up for the benefit of mankind. I ask that the crystals be blessed to release all negative vibrations to the universe to be dispersed without harm to any living thing.

Working with Crystals

Before working with your crystals follow the basic steps:

1. Protect and ground yourself
2. Cleanse and bless the crystal
3. Centre yourself by sitting with your eyes shut and concentrate on your breathing for a few moments.

If working with a single crystal, hold the crystal in your right hand with any point on the crystal towards your fingers, asking that you release all negative vibrations without harm to any living thing.

Now place the crystal into your left hand with the point towards your wrist and ask for the specific help you require. Work with the crystal in each hand for at least ten minutes.

Crystal Healing Techniques
Explore Your Crystal

When you first acquire a new crystal you should spend time exploring it. You will find that this develops your sensitivity to its energy field.

Step 1 Look at your crystal from different angles, close your eyes and hold it in both hands noting any thoughts you have.

Step 2 Hold the crystal in both hands and breath in imagining the air entering through the crystal and gently breath out over the crystal so that you have a cycle of breath going through the crystal, thus building energy.

Step 3 Sit quietly with your eyes closed and focus on the colour you can see, how the crystal feels in your palms and sense any vibrations or thoughts that cross your mind.

Step 4 Lie down and place the crystal on your solar plexus and sense how it feels, again visualise the colour of the crystal, the shape and any thoughts you pick up on.

Do this again with the crystal on your third eye, notice any changes.

Amazing Insight Into Crystal Healing

Crystal Healers

As an alternative healing method, or as some people call a holistic technique, or strengthening the body and mind, crystal healers have been around for thousands of years. Using various patterns utilizing natural crystals, a crystal healer's work with the aura of a body helps it to heal it in some way, whether physical or emotional. Sometimes referred to as gemstone therapy, the use of crystal healers is as widely varied as the gems that are employed in this technique.

Crystal healers learn how to heal a mind and body by playing the crystals on areas on the body known as chakras. A chakra is a term that refers to the spiritual energy that is present in everyone.

With seven major chakras throughout the body, each chakra works together to form aperson's energy and when that is out of alignment it can bring bad or negative energy to a person either in the mind or body. The crystals redirect the negative energy and instead direct the flow of good energy back into the body which in turn brings back the balance that the chakras naturally have. Ultimately, crystal healers use these gems to heal medical ailments, emotional discrepancies, and spiritual misguidance.

This History of Crystal Healers

Crystal healers have been found in almost every culture throughout history from the Indian tribes to the Egyptian people. Although the actual originator of using crystals as phsycial and mental therapy is unknown, it has been proven that this technique has been practiced for centuries and is still being used today all around the world. Even King Tut's tomb was surrounded by jade amulets which are thought to guide the soul after death. The Chinese culture still greatly believe in the use of crystal healers, especially with the use of jade and emerald which is thought to increase their memory and intelligence. In other cultures crystal healers would use agate, lapis lazuli, all types of amulets, amethyst and more to help with everything from sickness to stress.

The Benefits Crystal Healers Give to You

has a great number of benefits to help the spiritual nature of a person as well as mental and physical ailments. Some of the most powerful benefits to crystal healing are the use of crystal therapy for personal development as well as health and vitality. healers work with you to promote change within your self and your mind and to heal many physical conditions when conventional medicine just doesn't seem to work or it needs to be combined with holistic practices in order to spur on the recovery. Other ways that a crystal healer can benefit you is by relieving overall stress, anxiety and depression, or just helping you to relax. It can help with menstrual problems, headaches, digestive problems, relief from pain, fatigue, memory loss, concentration and even learning difficulties. It has shown great results with relationships, wealth building and personal self fulfillment.

By working to heal the body, crystal therapy is a natural form of deep relaxation mixed with meditation that boosts the overall immune system and makes the body function more efficiently. It benefits the body by balancing the mind with the spirit which in turn balances the body. It can boost creativity, improve communication and even help with the development of your spirituality. It is not recommended that you replace medical treatment if it is needed, but it can give a boost to your wellbeing that can actually improve the body and mind. From increasing feelings of empowerment, inspiring love, or to relieving migraines, healers offer a world of benefits to anyone.

What Crystal Healers Do

The act that a crystal healer performs is very simple. They place crystals on different parts of the body, in a certain area of a room or anywhere that corresponds to the chakras that are out of balance. By constructing an energy grid of sort to remove the bad energy and bring in the good energy, crystal healers work to surround a person with the healing energy that they need. This in turn removes the blocked chakras in the aura of the body. By using the color of crystals that match up with the color of the chakra, the crystals give off different healing vibrations for different treatments. This brings about the positive vibrations that attract positive events in the life of a person who uses a healer.

Crystal healers work in a place of serenity, usually in a space that promotes peace and quiet as well as comfort. Fully clothed, the healer will speak to you about what you feel is wrong so that they can decipher what crystals should be used and what chakras need to be unblocked. Some of the most popular gems healers use is amber, selenite, rose lepidolite, and subilite although there are many to choose from. Each offers a different healing property. For example, amber helps with the energy that helps with love and self esteem whereas the selenite helps the unblock energy of a person's higher consciousness. Crystal healers help a person to heal themselves from within and it is a skill that everyone can learn. In fact, there are several crystal healers' course workshops that promote the overall knowledge of how crystal healing can effectively change a person's life and wellbeing. During these crystal healers course workshops a person can learn how to use visualization techniques as well as relaxation techniques to help them remove the negative energy from their bodies and balance the chakras to again feel the positive energy move throughout the body.

Crystals - Frequently Asked Questions

What are the main benefits of crystals?

Crystals are decorative, potent and fascinating. They have magical powers and properties. They generate, store, regulate, transmit and transform energy - a quartz crystal can run a watch or a radio and crystal lasers are now being used in surgery. Putting out 'good vibes' crystals harmonize the atmosphere, or your body. Taking in energy, they cleanse the environment and your aura, and provide protection. Many crystals, such as Black Tourmaline or Amazonite, have a structure that absorbs energy. This means that the crystal holds onto detrimental energies such as electromagnetic 'smog', or negative thoughts and ill-wishing, and counteracts the detrimental effect. Crystals can be programmed to radiate 'good vibes' out into your environment, which makes them ideal for enhancing your home, your car or workplace. They can attract prosperity, love, friendship and anything you can imagine into your life. The ability of crystals to focus energy means that they can be used for specific tasks, such as directing healing energy to a point on the body or to an emotional blockage. Crystals divine the future and much more. By harnessing the unique beauty of crystals you can change your life. They can bring you everything your heart desires - if you know how to access their power. Crystals are often used for healing. Healing, in this respect, does not mean 'to make better', it means to improve well being and to make you feel good, although, in ancient and medieval times, crystals were actually ground up and administered as medicines.

Have our ancestors shaped the way crystals are used today?

Absolutely. Crystals have been used for thousands of years not only for adornment but also for healing and to influence the course of life. Ancient peoples believed crystals were gifts from the gods and that they actually carried the essence of a god or goddess. Amber beads have been found in graves over 8000 years old, for instance, and amber is still used as a protective stone today. Their magical properties have been recognised in every culture and were used by shamans, healers, magicians and astrologers so there's an enormous body tradition behind their use today. I'm doing a masters degree in Cultural Astronomy and Astrology and am researching the origins of birthstones as a follow on to my book The Crystal Zodiac. I'm presently back in ancient Mesopotamia, about 4000 years ago, and some of the birthstones were already in use then to attract the favour of the gods and to provide healing - hematite, which contains iron, was sacred to Mars and was used to treat blood conditions, exactly as today. In ancient Egypt crystals formed an important part of medical practice. In India, the Vedic remedial gems associated with the planets have been used for at least 3000 years and probably much longer.

How can people discover the magic of crystals and gemstones in their everyday life?

Crystals come in all shapes and sizes. Some are shining, glamorous - and sometimes expensive. Others are rough pieces, seemingly dull - until you know their secrets. A diamond or ruby could be overlooked in its raw state. Many stones are tumbled, cut or faceted to enhance their appearance, but work just as well in their natural form. So you can easily slip a crystal into your pocket or under your pillow and let it do its work.

For a crystal to work its magic, it must be magnetised to your energies. This aligns the crystal to your intent. It helps focus upon precisely what you want your crystal to do and ensures that the crystal will carry out its task. It is intention that makes magic work. Dedicating a crystal greatly enhances the effectiveness of the crystal and ensures that good comes from its use. Take it home, run it under the tap to cleanse its energies, and then hold it in both hands and programme it to respond to you by dedicating it to your specific purpose.

Love radiates out from many crystals and stones can be gently romantic as in the case of Rose Quartz or powerfully erotic like Red Jasper. They attract a soulmate or put a zing into an existing relationship. Crystals change how you feel about yourself, making you more open to love. You can feel love radiating out from many crystals and, worn over the heart, such stones can be very soothing. They have a gentle energy that helps you to accept and love yourself - a prerequisite to being loved by someone else. One of the most enjoyable ways to experience crystal love is to take a bath with your favourite stone. Choose one that radiates out the qualities you seek: passion, romance, self-love, healing for your heart, for instance. Cleanse the crystal and place it in the water, to which you can add a few drops of rose oil. Take a long, hot soak and absorb the energies. If you share the bath with your partner, so much the better. At night, slip the stone under your pillow to reinforce its effects.

Any other advice for first time crystal and gemstone users?

The crystal that speaks to you is the one for you. A crystal does not have to be expensive or rare to be effective. Size and appearance matter little when it comes to crystal power. Don't be fooled by bright, shiny and big. These are not necessarily the most effective. Small, misshapen and less attractive crystals often have the same power - and cost a great deal less. When you visit a crystal shop, notice which crystal catches your eye first. It will probably be the one for you. If you are looking for aspecific crystal, plunge your hand into a tub and the one that sticks to your hand has your name on it.

Remember that every body is different - we all radiate different frequencies, we have different attitudes, different family patterns. So there is no one magic 'cure all' crystal (although the many varieties of Quartz come close!). What works for you won't necessarily work for your friend, but there will be another one that does. So don't be afraid to experiment and to use crystals intuitively rather than following what someone else tells you is the way to do it - having said that, I've written several books to help you find the right way for you.

And remember also that many seemingly simple illnesses are really 'dis-eases'. There is an underlying emotional, mental or spiritual condition that is manifesting as an illness to draw your attention to itself. Crystals gently address these underlying conditions and bring you back into holistic balance: which the definition of healing I prefer.

One very important thing, crystals absorb negative energies so they need regular cleaning otherwise they become overstressed and stop working. The easiest way to do this is to hold them under running water for a few minutes and then put them out in the sun to recharge. They can also be put into brown rice or salt (but not if they are layered or friable) overnight or placed on a large Quartz cluster or Carnelian to cleanse and re-energise.

Are crystals and gemstones finally being recognised for the wonderful advantages they can offer?

Yes, I think the success of my books such as the Crystal Bible shows that more and more people are recognising the value of crystals. In England nowadays virtually every town has a crystal shop and they all report people coming in asking for a stone to take away a headache, attract love and so on, which is why, in addition to The Crystal Healing Pack, I've also compiled Crystal Prescriptions which gives you healing stones for every possible ailment and desire.

Life Healing Energy With Crystals

For years, many people used crystals in jewelry for the shear beauty of them. Crystal Healing is considered by many a pseudo scientific alternative medicine technique that employs stones and crystals for healing but is an ancient practice that dates back to at least 6,000 years. The Romans used crystals as talismans to promote good health and provide for protection in battle. Roman and Greek doctors mixed crystals with plant extracts, heated them, and used medicinally. Ancient Egyptians believed these stones had the power to restore health, and would also bury their dead with a quartz crystal, which they believed would guide their loved one safely to the afterlife. Chinese used them to promote healing, enlightenment, and attraction of desires.

Today, healers, Shamans, and priests use crystals for their specific healing properties. I always had a fascination with stones and crystals but that was as far as it ever went, until I was introduced to crystals and their healing ability at a Mind, Body, & Spirit Festival. Because crystals vibrate with the energy of the earth, they can help you align your body with the Earth's energy. With these crystals, now you too, may vibrate at the highest energy - Earth Energy! This is where the healing begins. Using crystals, and tuning yourself into their energy, you are then clearing blockages within you which will enhance your own natural healing powers. Most don't realize, but our bodies were designed to be self correcting and naturally heal themselves. But as life happens, we sometimes forget to stop and take care of ourselves so often, that our bodies get out of sync with that healing process, ultimately creating blockages in our physical and mental bodies.

Any blockages within your life force is what causes aches, pains, and even disease to manifest in the physical body. It's for this reason, I now use crystals every day for strength in a particular area in my life, for healing that's needed that day, for personal meditation and clarity, or for use in my Reiki practice to induce love and light while cleaning and clearing Chakras. Reiki, as just one alternative healing modality, in it's simplest translation is Universal Life Force. It is the practice of channeling the universal life energy in a particular pattern to heal and harmonize the mental and physical body and each of our Chakras, which receives, assimilates, and transmits physical, emotional, and spiritual energy flowing through our bodies. There is a clearing technique I use, as well as a different specific crystal for each Chakra to clear any and all blockages in that area. This clears the way for life force energy to flow to you and through you to keep the mind, body, and spirit in it's divine state of perfect health. If we keep our mind, body, and spirit vibrating on a high frequency of love and healing energy, we don't allow aches, pains, and disease to manifest and settle in the physical body.

This is just a brief overview on Chakra healing with crystals. Each crystal has its own unique healing property and a specific Chakra it resonates with due to its color. Our first Chakra, being the Root Chakra, deals with grounding, and mainly vibrates with and can be healed using Red, Brown, or Black Crystals such as Red Garnet, Hematite & Black Tourmaline. Our second Chakra, the Sacral Chakra, dealing with the abdomen and pleasure centers, can mainly be harmonized with Orange Crystals, such

Carnelian, Amber, and Orange Calcite. The Third Chakra, being the Solar Plexus Chakra, dealing with the Digestive System and personal power, resonate with and can be healed with Yellow Crystals like Yellow Citrine, and Sunstone. The Fourth Chakra, the Heart Chakra, deals with the Heart, Lungs, and Love. The Heart Chakra vibrates in a healing manner with all Green or Pink crystals such as Rose Quartz, Jade, or Green Aventurine. The fifth Chakra, the Throat Chakra, deals with communicating, and resonates with Blue Crystals such as Blue Agate, Sodalite, or Sapphire. The sixth Chakra, the Third Eye Chakra, dealing with intuition and knowing, vibrates on a healing level with Violet Crystals such as Amethyst, Lolite, & Flourite. The seventh Chakra, the Crown Chakra, dealing with the Central Nervous System & the Divine, resonates best with White or Purple Crystals such as Selenite, Clear Quartz, or Amethyst.

I've personally been using Crystals for my own healing for quite a bit, but since beginning the use of crystals for healing, I've had a few phenomenal success stories, some of which are near and dear to my heart. The first success story is my husband who had rotator cuff surgery. This, from what I'm told by many people, is the most painful surgery you can have. This is definitely an issue with a long healing time as he's only gained about three quarters of his motion back in that area without pain so far in the last 5 months. Initially, I would Reiki him while we were sitting and relaxing and the end of each day. Then I brought a Carnelian ball into the picture and what he explained to me while using the healing ball was pretty amazing. The Carnelian ball brought him amazing heat, almost like a hot stone everywhere it touched him helping to relax and heal the muscles that had been severed and manipulated during surgery, soothing the pain just like a hot stone massage.

The second success story is also near and dear to me as it has to do with my sister. My sister Deneen has Lupus, which is essentially an inflammatory disease where your body's immune system attacks its own tissue and organs. From what I hear and see her going through, it is a very painful disease and doctors just throw different medications at it as a trial and error thing until they find a drug that works. Well, she's still in a stage of her disease of not knowing what medication works in helping the pain which she endures every day. I've done Reiki healing on her numerous times in the past which has eased the pain just enough to take the edge off, but it wasn't until I started Crystal Healing Therapy, that she's had sustained relief from the pain. I used various different Crystals to Cleanse and Clear her Chakra's, but I also asked her to wear a Reiki Charged Hematite bracelet for a few hours a day. It's been a few weeks and she's reported not having had a really bad pain day since.

My third success story in just a few short weeks has to do with someone that has degenerative disc disease which is pain in the lower back or neck due to a compromised disc in the spine. While there is a slightly genetic cause to this disease, it's mainly caused by normal wear and tear or some sort of trauma to the body. With this type of disease, there is normally a constant, usually a slight baseline pain. It also involves mild to severe episodes of back or neck pain that generally could last anywhere from a few days to a few months and can be debilitating during that time, before returning the person back to what they consider their norm in the pain department. Rachael had been suffering for many many years with degenerative disc disease when she came to me. I helped her with the healing energy of Reiki and a Carnelian ball, which

I used to treat lower back problems. After those two things, I used Hematite on her which, for her, was like the Belle of the Ball. As soon as the Hematite stones made contact with the skin on her lower back, she reported a dissolving of the pain almost immediately and stayed for as long as the Hematite stayed on her back. I then instructed her to continue this practice on her own while she was not with me and to cleanse the Hematite with a Selenite stone so that all of the negativity and toxins the Hematite absorbed from her, would be cleared before returning them to her lower back again.

So despite the documented healing crystal use of many of our ancestors, some still discredit the use of these stones along with other forms of alternative medicine. There are not many studies to prove or even disprove the power of alternative forms of medicines such as crystal healing, acupuncture, Reiki, or even yoga as healing for the mind, body & spirit. This does not mean that these healing practices aren't effective. It just means that money isn't being spent on what some consider to be "New Age" healing; that same healing therapy that is actually healing as old as time. Also, despite the lack of research for these types of healing methods, still about one third of Americans use these or other forms of alternative medicine. This is not to say that Crystal Healing Therapy is a cure all. You should still seek the help and medical attention from your doctors, but as you can see from these three very different issues and diseases from the above cases, Crystal Healing Stones truly do serve to amplify any and all efforts of healing; whether you have emotional wounds, specific physical illness, or simply need to increase your energy levels, you can use crystals to vibrate with the same frequencies of earths energy and re-activate your body's very own healing capabilities!

Using Crystals With Reiki

Once you have learned the basic techniques of Reiki, you are encouraged to learn more about crystals and see if they resonate with you in your healing sessions.

Crystals can be placed directly on a patient or within their aura. They can also be used around the house for purification, near your computer to absorb electronic energy, to absorb pollutants and absorb natural radiation.

You can strategically place crystals around your house for neutralizing geopathic stress and negative environmental energies. Crystals can be worn as jewelry around your neck or carried in your pocket. You can also submerge crystals in your bottles of drinking water to strengthen and purify it.

I employ crystals in most, but not all of my healing sessions. If I sense that somebody would be skeptical of crystals, I'm much less likely to use them. On the other hand, some patients are really keen on discovering more about crystals, so I use them more liberally.

At the earth chakra located just below the feet, place a grounding stone such as hematite or smoky quartz. I generally do this during every healing because these stones are helpful for collecting any negative energy swept from the patient's aura during healing. It's especially important to cleanse these stones after each healing, as they function as a receptacle for negative or unwanted energy.

Many crystals can be effectively used on each of the chakras. I've included just a few to give you a taste of the variety and diversity of healing stones available to us here on earth. For the root chakra, smoky quartz assists in grounding and purifying. You can also choose a crystal such as red carnelian which is a stabilizing stone that also promotes self-trust. Red jasper grounds energy and can also be used for healing the circulatory, digestive and sexual organs.

If your patient has specific issues to heal, choose crystals for their specific healing characteristics. Once again, let me remind you to cleanse your healing crystals after each use. Run them under fresh water or rinse them with salt water. You can also hold them in your hands to energize and purify them. With Reiki 2, visualize the Cho Ku Rei and Sei He Ki symbols penetrating and empowering each stone. Finally, you can place your crystals in the sunshine to gather the energy of the sun and further purify them.

For the sacral chakra, choose red jasper for healing of sexual organs and enhancing sexual relationships. Orange calcite effectively balances the emotions, removes fear and helps overcome depression. It's used for healing the reproductive system, gallbladder and intestinal disorders such as irritable bowel syndrome.

Over the long term, study a book on crystals and learn the specific qualities of each stone. Purchase those stones that most resonate with you and incorporate them into your healing. Most often, I allow my intuition to select the stone for each healing. Call it laziness if you must, but I simply bring out my tray of healing stones, let my hand hover over the crystals until I feel naturally directed to select a few for my patient. Indeed, I'm employing basic knowledge of crystals such as knowing which color is suitable for each chakra, but I also trust my hand and heart to select stones that resonate with me at that moment.

Yellow tourmaline stimulates the solar plexus and is helpful to enhance personal power. Physically, it treats the stomach, liver, spleen, kidneys and gallbladder. Another beautiful stone is the tiger's eye which works on strengthening self worth, manifesting the will and overcoming self criticism. Generally, crystals of a yellow or golden hue are suitable for placement on the solar plexus chakra.

While scanning your patient's body at the beginning of a healing, you may find a blockage or weakness at one of the chakras. In this case, place the crystal directly on the chakra throughout the healing. The crystal then functions as your "third hand" throughout the duration of the healing process. When doing this, many people report that they feel my hand on one of their chakras long after I have moved to a different healing position.

I normally place a rose quartz on the heart chakra. The first stone that I fell in love with was a rose quartz and I carried it with me all the time. I used it in practically every healing. Finally, realizing that I had grown attached to it, I decided to give it to a good friend. It was the finest gift I had in my possession and sharing it with a close friend was the most important thing I could do with it. Rose quartz symbolizes unconditional love, purifying the heart at all levels including love of self. As you strengthen your love of self, you will automatically attract loving relationships into your life.

Rhodonite is another pink colored stone that can be placed directly on the heart chakra, or just above it. Rhodonite heals emotional wounds, facilitates forgiveness and transmutes painful emotions. Green stones such as green tourmaline, green quartz and moss agate can also be used effectively when working on the heart.

It would be very uncomfortable if you placed a crystal directly on the throat. It's better to place your chosen crystals below the throat or to one side. I normally use a blue quartz that I acquired in the mystical town of Capilla del Monte in central Argentina. I use it specifically for healing throat issues. For a long time, this was my personal favorite stone, so I always carried it in my pocket. As I got used to it (and it attuned to me), I felt confident using it in most healings. This shows that confidence in the healing power of a crystal, plus regular association with it, empowers you and your crystals to be more effective at healing.

More recently, I've begun using a lapis lazuli that my wife brought back for me from the sacred mountains of Pushkar in Rajasthan, India last year. I first heard of lapis lazuli in the epic poem by W.B. Yeats where he describes the power of the arts and artisans, which coincidentally relate to the creative aspects of the throat chakra. Although I don't know if Yeats was familiar with the healing qualities of lapis lazuli, he was certainly attracted to the beauty and imaginative characteristics of this visionary stone. Lapis lazuli balances the throat chakra and heals the throat, larynx, thyroid and thymus. It is said to encourage self awareness and strengthen self expression, the major issues of the throat chakra. Lapis makes beautiful jewelry that can attractively and therapeutically be worn around the neck.

On the brow chakra, lapis lazuli can also be used to stimulate enlightenment, enhance psychic ability and guide you on your spiritual path. In my own practice, I generally use purple amethyst during meditation, when healing myself and healing others. My first experience with this crystal was when my friend Ken visited from England. He had been using amethyst in his healing work for decades, and this was the stone he selected as a gift for me. Amethyst has a high spiritual vibration. It strengthens common sense, spiritual insight, intuition and psychic ability. It's always suitable for use on the brow chakra.

Purple amethyst is also useful on the crown chakra because it connects the physical, mental and emotional bodies with the spiritual. It cleanses the aura and transmutes negative energy. Overall, it's one of the most spiritual stones. If I had to recommend a single stone for your healing and meditation practice, I would suggest amethyst.

If you decide to purchase stones for your own use, visit a gem shop and examine their inventory. Pick up any stone that you find attractive and hold it in your hand to sense its energy. If it resonates with you, it just might be your stone. Discuss the qualities of the stone with the merchant or study more about its healing and esoteric qualities. Using a combination of intuition, knowledge and touch, you will discover the crystals most suitable for you. You can also bring your pendulum with you to the gem shop and use it to read which crystals are most in tune with your personal energy.

On a concluding note, be aware of the shapes, sizes and processes that go into crystals. You will find highly polished stones that make beautiful pendants, but to me, all that polishing and processing distract from the pure, natural aesthetics of the stone. Thus, I much prefer a rough, unpolished stone just as it was found in the earth. On the other hand, crystals can be very artistically crafted into wands, spheres or hearts.

Crystal Healing: New age "Hooey" Or Truth?

To most of us, who have spent our lives grounded in the physical plane that we like to call "reality", the idea of crystal healing has made it's way into the category of irrational superstition and "new age hooey". It's as if most of us are asking, how in the world can a rock be anything more than a rock much less store energy or help us heal? How can rocks, minerals and metals do anything but just sit there?

To answer this question, we must venture beyond the physical existence which we currently think is "all there is" to this reality we are living in.

Physical matter has long been seen as the stable basis of reality. In other words, physicality is the test most of us use to determine what is "real" from what is "not real". But physical matter is not the center of reality as we know it. Instead, it is only a tiny aspect of infinite energy within the universe. You could think of physical reality like the thin, outermost membrane of this universe, much like skin. A layer of epidermis, covering an unseen substructure of other vast dimensions where energy is expressed differently because it vibrates at different frequencies depending on the dimension it exists in. Every single physical object whether it is living or not living exists not only in this physical level, but also in the multitude of energetic dimensions outside physicality. Everything you see in this world is multidimensional in nature. Your entire bodily system is nothing more than energy that shows up in various patterns and densities. The same goes for what we consider to be "inanimate structures" like rocks.

When patterns of energy work together in a non resistant and cohesive way then we experience what we call health. These patterns of energy can be disrupted by a multitude of things. When this happens we experience a state of dis-ease. This leads to poor health. This resistant, discordant energy patterning is responsible for every negative symptom we experience in our physical from, everything from a headache to cancer.

Everything we believe is solid and "real" is simply appearing real to us because of our physical senses, but our physical senses are doing nothing more than interpreting energy as a scent or as a sight or a taste of a feel. It is our senses which convert what is for lack of a better word an energetic, holographic reality into the static reality we call physical. It is our senses that tell us that we are "separate" from our surroundings. At our most fundamental level, we are not only participating in this vast energetic field, we are also made of this energetic field. We are one with every animate and inanimate thing we see. Our physical lives are only different expressions of the very same energy which makes up "all that is" across every universe and in every dimension. The amplitude and frequency (what we often call vibration) at which this energy expresses itself, is what determines whether energy becomes a person or a rock in the physical dimension.

Crystals and what we call gemstones, have a vibration which is free of resistant patterns. They are among some of the structures in the physical dimension which have the very most balanced, cohesive, strong and intentional frequencies. Their un-changing physical structure is a reflection of the fact that their innate energetic patterns of balance and strength and cohesiveness are incorruptible. In the physical dimension when you pick up a crystal it may look like you are not really doing more than touching and looking at a separate, physical object. But in the other dimensions in which both you and the rock exist, you are "entraining" energetically with that rock. This entrainment then causes changes to your structure and psychology on the physical dimension. The governing law of every dimension within the universe is that of "oneness". In physical life, we have come to call this the "Law of Attraction". Simply put, only frequencies which are a vibrational match can co-exist. Therefore, in order to share the same space with another "form", you must be vibrating at the same level as it is vibrating. Health is the natural state of any form within the universe. Therefore the natural inclination and tendency of anything within the universe is that of balance, cohesiveness and ease. This means that the natural progression of vibration is to entrain and resonate in the direction of health. Because of this, when you share the space a crystal (or gemstone) which has a resistance free vibration, instead of the vibration of the crystal adopting a non cohesive pattern, your energy will entrain with the energy of the crystal and adopt it's cohesive pattern. This entrainment, causes you to no longer create the pattern of dis-ease within your energetic substructures and therefore the physical manifestation of that dis-eased energy is no longer being maintained and the physical symptom disappears. Because of this entrainment effect, crystals and gemstones are incredibly adept at bringing us back into a vibrational state of health and harmony. Anything with an inherent energetic pattern of non resistance can act like a tuning fork by offering a vibration which we can use to re-tune ourselves to a healthy vibration. This is what is really happening on the energetic levels of substructure when you listen to a song that makes you feel good, or spend time near a person that makes you feel good, or take a homeopathic remedy.

Each crystal or gemstone resonates with a slightly different pattern energetically, and therefore (just like our specific physical structures), appears different in the physical in terms of things like chemical composition, structure, geometry, color and texture. Because of this, each one lends itself to patterns which reside in our specific physical systems. For example, to share the space with rose quartz is to expose the energetic patterns active in our physical and metaphoric heart to align themselves with health and adopt a more resistance free pattern. Therefore, when we entrain with rose quarts, unresolved heart issues will dissipate, allowing us to let go of whatever is distorting our energies which identify with the heart.

Crystals and gemstones grow deep within in the earth's crust over millions of years at extremely high pressures and heat. This gives them a place among the objects on earth with the very most inherent energy. They are capable of receiving, containing, projecting, emanating, refracting, and reflecting energy. Crystals have a very consistent arrangement of atoms. In the gem stone called "quartz" these atoms vibrate at a stable and measurable frequency, because of this, quartz an excellent receiver and emitter of electro-magnetic energy. Because of this, quartz is used in radios, watches, and numerous electronic technologies. Nobel prize-winning scientist Marcel Vogel discovered that not only can crystals be programmed as silicon chips in a computer, but they also can be programmed with the energy of consciousness. He discovered that when a person uses a computer, thoughts are directed to the computer by pressing on the keyboard, that information is stored in the computer's silicon chips via the medium of electricity. Vogel then reasoned correctly that like electricity, thought is a form of energy which can be given direction by what we call "intention". He concluded due to this discovery that crystals could also be programmed without the need for electricity, by using just thoughts as the informational energy.

Quartz is what is called a piezoelectric material. A piezoelectric substance is something that produces an electric charge when a mechanical stress is applied. When piezoelectric material is placed under mechanical stress, a shifting of the positive and negative charge centers in the material takes place, which then results in an external electrical field. This stress can be caused by hitting or twisting the material just enough to deform its crystal lattice without fracturing it. The effect also works in the opposite way, with the material deforming slightly when a small electric current is applied. While the argument rages back and forth as to whether the piezoelectric effect plays a role in the human-crystal healing relationship or not, the fact that crystals are so responsive to electro-magnetic fields has serious implications. It has serious implications because our bodies are composed of and constantly emanating electro-magnetic fields and crystals and gemstones respond to this electricity that is creating and coursing through our bodies. Another interesting finding is that quartz is composed of silicon and oxygen ($SiO2$), a combination known to geologists as the building block of all minerals. Our planet is made up of minerals containing silicon and oxygen. Silicon is an important constituent of our human bodies. Some of the more science oriented people have theorized that the transfer of energy from the natural crystal to the silicon within our own bodies could have something to do with the physical healing effect caused by exposure to crystals.

Crystals and Gemstones are one of the most powerful tools available to us in the physical dimension of existence. It is a tool all of us have used subconsciously at one time or another. Often it's an interaction that takes place by our attention being drawn to a specific rock. On the physical level, we think it is "pretty" and though we do not know why we like it so much, we feel compelled to pick it up and keep it in our pocket. We have no idea why we felt this urge and we have no conscious awareness of what is behind our impulse to pick it up. We have no idea that our energetic substructure is calling us towards the specific vibration of that rock in order to entrain with it and move towards a more cohesive healthy pattern than the one we are currently maintaining within ourselves. Like all tools, the key to maximum utilization is to learn how to consciously implement the tool. If this a fore mentioned scenario could cross over from a subconscious compulsion to a conscious process of seeking out a specific crystal or gemstone based on knowledge of the benefit of using it, the person's receptivity would be such that the effects of the entrainment would be a hundred fold. If we consciously recognized that our own electro-magnetic fields are impacted by the energetic quality of each crystal and gemstone, we would see that they create an electro-chemical response within our body and psychology which would allow us to use them as the powerful tools that they are. We could use them on a daily basis to promote health, awareness, growth and evolution within ourselves and the multidimensional lives we lead.

Crystal-Healing The Chakras: A Practical Guide

Who among us really understands the chakras? For all that we know about these seven spinal energy points, much is still undiscovered.

According to ancient texts, the chakras appear as spinning wheels of light. In fact, the word chakra is Sanskrit for wheel. Chakras receive and emit energy, which may be either negative or positive depending on the health of this energy. During the healing process, you will discover differences in the needs of each chakra. You needn't fear this challenge. Think of your chakras as a garden, with each flower requiring specialized care. Some chakras will require less attention, while others are more demanding. The dedication to this self-scrutiny makes healing the chakras as challenging as it is rewarding.

The guidelines below may be modified to your needs. When choosing stones, be attentive not to the size or appearance, but instead to your reaction when holding them. Some of these crystals may be unfamiliar, but you are likely to find them at a metaphysical or rock shop. Though you may enjoy this introduction to chakra healing, it is best to undertake long-term treatment with the guidance of a trained professional. Besides being experienced, many professional chakra healers are highly intuitive. Their objective insight may help you understand the reasons for each imbalance. This can be healing in and of itself.

1st Chakra:This is the root chakra. It is located at the base of your spine, or tailbone. The root chakra belongs to the realm of the physical. If you feel grounded, secure, and rooted in the present, this chakra needs little attention. However, many are not so blessed. A blocked root chakra may lead you to grasp at the physical, becoming clingy and overly possessive. Conversely, if you're too open here you may feel estranged from your body and possessions. As a result, your generosity may be taken advantage of. Crystal Correction:A blocked chakra is opened by obsidian. This gem brings a centered, peaceful perspective, so that the impulse to compulsively acquire is replaced by an understanding of the temporary nature of belongings. To heal blocks, place a piece of obsidian on your genital region while lying down on your back, As you relax more the stone's strength will connect with your own, enhancing it. An abundantly open root needs rose quartz. Though typically associated with the heart, this soft pink quartz allows us to accept and love ourselves, so we can protect ourselves by saying no.

2nd Chakra:The sacral chakra controls our sexual energy and creativity. You need only press two inches below your navel to feel its location. The gift of a balanced sacral chakra is expressiveness and flair. A blockage may result in resistance to new ideas. A sacral chakra that's too open is evident in the "drama queen" as well as in all reckless behavior, from bed-hopping to dangerous driving.

Crystal Correction: Carnelian: this variety of quartz is beautiful for opening the sacral area. Though it can be found in many colors, the stimulating qualities of red or orange give courage to the timid. This enables us to pursue our dreams, without fear-based illusions blocking our path. Conversely, if this chakra is too open, you may require lapis luizi. This historic light blue stone was highly valued in ancient Egypt and Babylon. Today, we can use its moderating properties to help us act with care. In

Crystal, Gems & Metal Magic, Scott Cunningham writes: "Simply touching the body with this stone improves your mental, physical, spiritual, psychic and emotional condition." For optimum benefits to the 2nd chakra, rest this stone as long as desired.

3rd Chakra: This is your solar plexus, known also as the power center. Here resides a reservoir of untapped will and heroism. When this chakra is healthy, we understand our potential and are motivated to explore it. When blocked we may feel "butterflies in our stomach" or suffer other stomach woes. A blocked power center makes us act and feel powerless. The opposite problem happens when this energy-center is too broad.

Crystal Correction: Golden Beryl is a light, lemon yellow stone that directs will and improves confidence. Consequently, it is fantastic for 3rd chakra blockages. Placing this stone two inches above your navel will free your power center, helping you to realize your goals. For those overwhelmed by this chakra, green jade is in order. This soothing stone helps channel our passions gently and harmlessly, and reduces negative impulses towards others.

4th Chakra: This is the heart chakra and its place is self-explanatory. This is the divine sphere of spiritual growth, love, resilience and high ideals. A congested heart chakra makes us overly critical of both others and ourselves. In this condition, we find it difficult to open ourselves to possibilities for love and friendship. Conversely, if our heart is too big, we may attempt to do the impossible, trying to carry the weight of the world.

Crystal Correction: Placed upon the heart, green jasper helps us feel secure enough to open up and reveal ourselves. This facilitates honest and joyful communication. For a heart with no bounds try peridot. This pale, pastel green stone also recharges us by calming us down. Peridot allows us to be sympathetic but not sacrificial.

5th Chakra:The throat chakra helps us communicate both through words and physical language. It is located at the base of the throat. When this chakra is balanced, we speak honestly and confidently. If we are blocked here, our deceit is subtle. For example, we may leave out information. Alternately, if this chakra is enlarged we talk too much and without forethought. This is commonly known as "foot in mouth" syndrome.

Crystal Correction: Sodalite;a gorgeous navy stone, helps with a constricted throat chakra. This crystal gives us courage and clarity. Knowing our truth, we may sound it with conviction. On the other hand, those with an expansive 5th chakra need to sound their truth more quietly. In this capacity, amber is helpful. This stone is intensely soulful. In The Crystal Handbook, Kevin Sullivan reveals that "in Viennese esoteric literature, Amber marked the resting place of the spirit or spirits believed to animate the stone." Fossilized, multimillion year-old tree sap, amber gifts us with the natural wisdom of early earth.

6th Chakra: Many know this energy center, located between the brows, as the 3rd eye. If in balance, this chakra gives us the ability to peer beyond appearances, revealing our innate psychic potential. When it is blocked, however, we limit ourselves to unexamined facts. This leads to rigid thinking and interrupted joy. However, if we are too open here we may be disconnected from the physical world. An inability to shut the psychic eye, when fitting, floods with an upsetting sense of unreality. Balance is key. As we dream, we also must wake

Crystal Correction:A moonstone placed on the 6th chakra can clear the issues that blind our intuition, and open the mind to the unseen. Because moonstone is related to cycles of change, it invites personal growth. This helps us tune into flow, welcoming spontaneity and releasing rigidity. With an unnecessarily open 3rd eye, blue lace agate is needed. This pretty, sky-blue stone sharpens our focus, clearing out the clutter of psychic distraction.

7th Chakra: Wow! Words are not enough to express the capacity of the crown chakra.. Situated at top-center of your head, this chakra presents the possibility of enlightenment. Though balancing it won't make us a Buddha, it will surely carry us to peaks of spiritual ecstasy and connect us with our life's purpose. If you're blocked here, you're far from alone. a healthy crown chakra is rare. It is the gift of tireless efforts in spiritual self-development. When blocked, we may be confused about our career and lack lasting, rapturous peace. For maximum results at balancing this chakra, we must first ensure the wellbeing of our previous chakras. Having this chakra too open is rarely a problem, unless you dislike joy and harmony. Yet, we live among the disenchanted. We must be able to communicate with both the cynic and the sorrowful. Otherwise we are trapped in our own mind. As safe as this place is, it can get pretty lonely.

Crystal Correction:Clear quartz is a trusted healer for all chakras, but it particularly useful in opening the closed crown. Due to the 7th chakras location, the crystal selected should be small enough to rest on the top of your head. This stone provides clarity of purpose and allows us to see the broader meaning in everyday events. In doing so, it guides us to understand and live in sync with universal truths. For those with an overly open crown chakra, hematite is healing. It is also grounding. By drawing attention to the practical realities of existence, this dark and powerful stone will help us meet our own and others earthly needs.

Sidebar: Discover Your Blocks with a Pendulum

Using a pendulum is a quick and reliable way to self-diagnose your chakra imbalances. To start, obtain a 6-sided quartz pendulum from a rope or chain. Many metaphysical shops carry these beauties. Hold this crystal steadily over the chakra you are most curious about. Soon, you will notice the crystal begin to move. Do not be concerned about the direction of the swing. On the contrary, width is what's important. An extremely wide swing indicates an overly open chakra, where a tight, shaky swing identifies a block.

Essential Basics Of Thin Film Deposition Control By Quartz Crystal Monitoring

Thin Film Deposition is a vacuum technology for applying coatings of pure materials to the surface of various objects. The coatings, also called films, are usually in the thickness range of angstroms to microns and can be a single material, or can be multiple materials in a layered structure. This paper discusses the basic principles of thickness and rate control by use of quartz crystal monitoring.

One major class of deposition techniques is evaporation, which involves heating a solid material inside a high vacuum chamber, taking it to a temperature which produces some vapor pressure. Inside the vacuum, even a relatively low vapor pressure is sufficient to raise a vapor cloud inside the chamber. This evaporated material condenses on surfaces in the chamber as a coating or "film". This method, including the general type of chamber designs commonly used for it, is an excellent candidate for successful control of rate and thickness through the use of quartz crystals.

The key concept behind this type of measurement and control is that an oscillator crystal can be suitably mounted inside the vacuum chamber to receive deposition in real time and be affected by it in a measurable way. Specifically the oscillation frequency will drop as the crystal's mass is increased by the material being deposited on it. To complete the measurement system, an electronic instrument continuously reads the frequency and performs appropriate mathematical functions to convert that frequency data to thickness data, both instantaneous rate and cumulated thickness.

Such sensors and instruments are readily commercially available, including in an integrated package that not only reads and displays the rate and thickness data, but also provides outputs for other deposition system elements. It will have an analog drive signal to drive the source power supply in a closed loop technique based on the rate data and thus is able to maintain a preset rate during deposition. And it will have other outputs to interface with functions such as a source shutter triggered to close when the preset final thickness is achieved.

We will not go into the technical details of the instrument itself, or the algorithms that convert frequency to thickness. But it is useful to remember that the actual physical measurement is frequency and the rest is mathematical interpretation based on certain assumptions, one of which is that all frequency changes are due solely to film thickness on the crystal face, which is not necessarily true. Such things as transient temperature changes of the crystal can also cause frequency changes and be misinterpreted as film thickness. Such transients are generally of finite duration, though, and have only a small overall effect on the measured deposition in most cases. You typically have a graph display of rate vs time while depositing, and if you see a surprising transient it could be caused by this temperature issue rather than actual deposition, such as a blast of heat hitting the crystal when the source shutter first opens.

There can be numerous physical configurations of evaporation process chambers, but one of the most common will have the evaporant material source/heat source at the bottom of the chamber, with its vapor stream to rise above it and deposit from the underside onto a rotating substrate holder/tooling (often called a 'dome' for its typical shape). There is normally a movable physical shutter above the source between it and the substrates. When open, the substrates as well as the crystal monitor are subjected to the deposition. When the shutter is closed, at least the substrates must be shielded from the deposition, and usually the crystal is, too. The crystal, with its electrical cable, cooling water lines, and mechanical elements are securely mounted in a suitable location with the face of the crystal aimed at the source.

Quartz crystal rate controllers typically allow you to program in a desired heat profile (in terms of source power rather than actual temperature as such) to pre-condition the material prior to opening the source shutter and beginning actual deposition. This profile is experimentally determined by the user is normally formatted to to some 'soak' level and for each source/material, and in the controller have two separate sequential ramps of power be held there for some time.

The first ramp up is usually slower and stops at some level just below vaporization and holds it to achieve an acceptable degree of equilibrium before making the second ramp up to vaporization. The latter should ideally be the actual power level for the desired deposition rate, and in most cases, since you will now be consuming material and coating the bottom of the shutter, this second ramp and soak is made fairly brief. But those details are user choices. The controller lets you decide how you want it.

Once the final soak is complete, the controller will open the shutter and transition to closed loop power control to hold the programmed deposition rate and continue until final programmed film thickness is achieved. At that time the shutter closes and the controller executes a user programmed cool down profile similar to the heat up one. The closed loop control is usually a PID controller with user control of the parameters including the option of not using all three - depending on the characteristics of the power source, P alone might work, for example. As mentioned earlier, the instrument usually offers a choice of data displays, the most popular being rate vs time.

There can be various other options in such controllers, such as establishing closed loop control at some deposition rate in angstroms per second, and then, remaining under such control, ramping the rate up (or down) to a new rate and continuing from there, still ultimately going to the final programmed thickness with potentially several different controlled rate segments along the way. a crystal has details to attend to, such as calibrating its thickness readings. It can, of course, only "see" the deposition that lands directly on itself, which is not what a user wants to know or to control. The user wants to know what is on the substrates, so physical measurements need to be made to compare to the crystal reading and a calibration factor (normally called "tooling" factor) needs to be calculated, programmed into the instrument, and then verified.

Another important point is that crystals do not last forever. A new crystal will have an initial operating frequency (most commonly 6.0 MHz), which will drop as material is deposited on the crystal. The oscillator hasq a lower limit of frequency at which it can perform, which is definitely one way for a crystal to fail. But it is not at all uncommon for a given crystal in actual use to never make it that far and to fail earlier from noise issues or other reasons.

To resolve angstroms of deposition, the oscillation has to be very good, and very stable and it does not take too much for the instrument to reject one as "failed". So make sure to order a supply of these vital consumables, and remember that the substrates inside being processed are undoubtedly much more valuable than a crystal so don't try to push for maximum life on a cheap crystal and risk scrapping a load of valuable product.

There are too many other aspects and options to cover them all in this essential basics article, but these quartz crystal rate monitors/controllers are used on virtually all evaporators, either filament/boat type or e-beam type. A major reason is the variability of deposition rate vs source drive power in most such systems - with these controllers you can better hold a rate and a thickness in spite of any such variation.

While it is possible to use this same crystal monitoring and control technology in a sputtering system, it is actually rarely done for several reasons, one of which is that deposition rate vs cathode drive power is usually adequately stable for process control in sputtering. Also, typical sputter chambers are less amenable to positioning crystals, and plasma can interfere with them.

Time Crystals And Society

The people appointed by governments to look after infectious diseases include highly trained epidemiologists. They have identified the existence of what they refer to as a global 3D epidemic transmitted by the mass manufacture of dysfunctional communication and information devices. They have no antidote to the sociological damage that the epidemic is causing. Not one of them could find a place in the United Nations to discuss an antidote to this neurological disorder, which leads to continual warfare on earth. As a result, despite years of endless United Nations meetings, resolutions and emotional expressions of moral outrage, the epidemic spreading across the planet is getting worse.

No apology is made for not writing about this subject in the language of incomprehensible, dysfunctional peer reviewed, technological scientific jargon. Papers of great importance related to various aspects of it do indeed exist. Modern science, in its euphoric lust for power, prestige and violence is simply unable and unwilling to comprehend its overall human survival implications. To the best of my knowledge there are no peer reviewed papers written about the crucial substance of this article. Its ethos is 'For the People by the People', which embraces humans as belonging to one species rather than various tribes dedicated to imposing scientific violence upon each other.

The antidote to the dysfunctional information epidemic has actually been discovered and internationally recognized. It is beyond the primitive understanding of the prevailing global scientific death cult, which is governed by a law demanding the extinction of all life in the universe - the second law of thermodynamics.

It is common knowledge that religious or bureaucratic persuasions written into political law direct the ethos of nationalistic governmental scientific research. If the living process belongs instead to an infinite fractal mathematical logic linked to artistic emotion then prevailing science and religion will only allow vague glimpses of its intuitive reality.

If one carefully watches the brilliant documentary by Arthur C Clarke entitled 'The Colours of Infinity' both Clarke and Benoit Mandelbrot, acclaimed as the discoverer of infinite fractal logic, exclude humanity from any infinite purpose. However, The NASA High Energy Project has published papers by Petar Grujic, Science Advisor to the Belgrade Institute of Physics, showing that ancient Greek science had linked the living process to concepts of an infinite fractal universe.

The dysfunctional information epidemic ignores such living infinite information. It is only interested in prolonging the tribal 'survival of the fittest' paradigm for the benefit of government by the wealthy. Plutocracies around the world play dysfunctional financial poker-machine-like games of war to supposedly protect the people they represent from falling under the control of foreign governments.

In simplistic terms, the mathematical programming within electromagnetic gambling devices (i.e. poker machines) are designed to cause states of eventual financial and moral bankruptcy. They use sound and colour vibrations capable of inducing illusory heroin-like addictions to bring bankruptcies about. Global stock markets over time can be observed to record that such financial war games are using dysfunctional mathematical deceit to outwit their competitors.

The ancient Greek political 'Science for ethical ends' on the other hand, developed a concept of evolution using the mathematics now associated with the creation of the time crystal. The mathematical movement of the 28 day moon cycle was thought to explain the emotional female fertility rhythm. This harmonic 'Music of the Spheres' movement resonated with the atoms of a mother's spirit to generate the ethics of her love and care for children. Her joy at anticipating artistic colourful costumes for her children is very real and can be shared with family and friends. This can be contrasted to the unreal hallucinatory joy associated with the mathematical deceit programmed into the poker-machine.

The ancient political science was to guide ennobling government for the health of an infinite universe, in order to prevent the extinction of civilization. That ideal about universal health is consistent with a futuristic medical science employing infinite fractal mathematics, rather than the prevailing primitive death cult mathematics, which demands that our evolutionary process must lead only to extinction.

During the 1980s Australian Science-Art researchers used the ancient Greek infinity mathematics to become the first institute in the world to measure the existence of the life-force. They programmed a computer to generate simulations of seashell growth and development through a period of 50 million years. The evolutionary seashell mathematics matched exactly with the mathematics written into the seashell fossil record. In 1990 the world's largest technological research institute, IEEE in Washington, published their findings as being one of the important optical mathematical discoveries of the 20th Century, placing it alongside such names as Louis Pasteur and Francis Crick.

Scientists, infected by our science of dysfunctional information, were unable to even begin to comprehend that the evolutionary mathematical writing within the world's seashell fossil record had been written by the living creature within the shell. It was not difficult to demonstrate that the modern scientific mind was infected with some emotional form of cancer, preventing any attempt to gain a mental visualization of infinite reality. This cancer is religious in nature. Permission from a chosen deity to obtain knowledge of infinity results in deadly conflict between and within differing tribal ideologies capable of leading to world war.

All this confusion can be resolved quite quickly by programming a computer to entangle death cult science with the antidote information in order to obtain scientific human survival blueprint simulations. In 1974 the founder of the American National Foundation for Cancer Research, the Nobel Laureate in Medicine, Szent-Gyorgyi, wrote his 'Letter to Science' explaining that the prevailing method of assessing scientific research was in itself a form of neurological cancer.

Proof exists that Szent-Gyorgyi was correct in stating that modern scientific research comprehension is carcinogenic in nature. If you replace the ancient infinite mathematics belonging to the seashell discovery with sterile quantum mechanical mathematics within a computer, the futuristic simulations become distorted, clearly depicting the nature of cancerous growth and development. Szent-Gyorgyi's cancer research together with the Australian seashell discoveries was an important step toward the discovery of the antidote for the dysfunctional information epidemic.

The recent creation of time crystals, a completely new form of matter, by Harvard University physicists and a University of Maryland research team, was recently published by the scientific journal Nature. The mysterious nature of time crystals was predicted in 2012 by the Nobel Laureate, Frank Wilczek. At an atomic scale the newly created time crystals function outside the law upholding our prevailing understanding of reality - the second law of thermodynamics.

However, the time crystals' discovery, as a display of incredible scientific brilliance is associated with an extremely serious problem, one that surely warrants further critical scientific examination. The creation of time crystals was heralded by the emotional proclamation that Issac Newton's world-view had been destroyed. From the perspective of our prevailing science this appears obvious, however, it is simply incorrect. Newton, in his published 28th Query Discussions, stated categorically that his non-mechanical description of the universe was derived from ancient Greek Science. That ancient 'Science for ethical ends' is compatible with the reality of the atomic time crystal.

The magnitude of this erroneous information is enormous. Newton wrote that the mass of bodies in space does not cause gravity and that those who taught this were advocating a pretentious illusory version of reality. The Church did not tolerate any other examination of infinite reality than its incomprehensible religious dogma, which Newton, a deeply religious Christian, totally despised.

It can be considered that this deceitful religious 17th Century pretense concerning gravitational force is one of the key building blocks used to develop the current 3D epidemic of dysfunctional information. However, a far more ancient use of deceitful religious mathematics emerged at the dawn of civilization in Mesopotamia. Ancient tribes fighting each other for survival needed to obey the 'survival of the fittest' paradigm in order to be able to evolve. Sexual excitement linked to a lust for waging war was the tribal criteria for such survival.

The ancient Sumerians used celestial movement to invent a mathematical measurement of time and direction, now used in our scientific exploration of the universe. However, their concept of infinity was religious rather that mathematical. From numerous ancient clay tablets, concepts involving various warlike gods and goddesses living within a dark abyss, declaring 'Let there be light' and then creating hybrid versions of humanity, exist. The concept of infinity belonged to an argument among the gods over the bestowing of immortal life to the keeper of the Ark during the Great Flood. The ancient Mesopotamian tribes had no option but to observe the 'survival of the fittest' paradigm. It was inevitable that existing Sumerian mathematics was also developed and placed into political law to appease their goddess of sex and war, Inanna.

The following Babylonian Kingdom developed variations of the Sumerian religious beliefs, later influencing Islamic, Hebrew and Christian religious thought. The Babylonians replaced

Inanna with their goddess of prostitution and war, Ishtar. They developed the astrological Sumerian mathematics to be able to predict eclipses. One existing clay tablet records that in 673 BC, a priest advised the King to terrorize the populace by predicting a lunar eclipse. The Gods demanded this information was to be used to incite a lust for war to extend the boundaries of the kingdom.

This code of 'survival of the fittest' military conduct was written into their legal system, aspects of which were later inherited by Roman law, and later still within the Western legal system. During the 19th Century, the American champion of Democratic thought, Ralph Waldo Emerson, wrote that the American Plutocrats had placed aspects of Babylonian law into the structure of American politics. As a result the American people had become enslaved into a perpetual system of financial debt. His solution to this problem was to develop a new industrial technology from Sanskrit mathematics, which allowed the living process to extend to infinity.

There is no disputing the great genius of Albert Einstein nor his compassionate artistic nature. Following the disclosure of his theory of relativity early in the 20th Century he spent the rest of his life attempting to complete quantum mechanics with a living component. The heart-rending tragedy belonging to that lonely quest has been recorded. The book entitled 'Babylonian Mythology and Modern Science' published by the New York University's Library of Science in 1957, stated that Einstein derived his theory of relativity from the mythological mathematical intuitions of ancient Babylon. His later work explained his attempts to modify this conviction and he spent most of his life speculating in vain on how he might embrace a living purpose to complete quantum mechanical science.

Newton's understanding of the universe was derived from ancient Greek Science. This ancient 'Science for ethical ends' is compatible with the reality of the atomic time crystal. Newton was referring to the Greek concept of infinity concerning Anaximander's infinite primordial substance, called Aperion. The philosopher of science, Karl Popper, wrote about the Apeiron concept. He stated, "In my opinion this idea of Anaximander's is one of the boldest, most revolutionary and most portentous ideas in the whole history of human thought."

Newton's belief that the Greek science was authentic and that the prevailing science of his time was pretentious in assuming that the mass of bodies in space was the cause of gravitational force, is most important. It clearly demonstrates that Quantum mechanics has been based upon the false assumption that Newton's understanding of the universe was entirely a mechanistic one. Newton considered that his balancing description of a non-mechanical cosmos was more profound than his mechanistic description of the universe. This coincides with Karl

Popper's consideration that this issue is of the utmost global importance, hence the significance of the antidote discovery.

Popper's concept that the ancient Greek science held the most important idea in the history of the world can be explained by its definition of the nature of political evil. Within Plato's book, The Republic, ethical political science warns that "Evil" belongs to the destructive property of unformed matter within the physical atom, which can emerge to destroy civilization. The building of the atomic bomb before the psychopathic German Third Reich did so, can be considered to be an ethical tribal necessity. However, scientists never thought about developing the ethical technologies that Platonic science had obviously alluded to. As a result the threat posed by atomic bombs has moved the Doomsday Clock a few minutes to the Doomsday hour. The creation of the atomic time crystal has now accelerated that situation. The intent to use the crystal's functioning within the present dysfunctional science of artificial intelligence can only bring about truly catastrophic damage. It can be considered that the global neurological cancer information epidemic will go terminal unless the antidote is developed.

If the time crystal physics reality is associated with the living information and communication devices recently discovered existing throughout the entire length of the DNA, then a wonderful human evolutionary survival technology will emerge. Artificial intelligence has no history of feelings associated with the evolution of ethical atomic compassion, but the human metabolism certainly has.

Plato used mathematics to explain how artistic emotional feelings were not ethical. This was because they were lacking an ethical spiritual component. An example of what he was referring to is not difficult to find. The ancient Roman legal system held that the mathematics used to build beautiful aqueducts to bring fresh water to the citizens of Rome was its symbol of power. It was noted that it was vastly superior to the mathematics that was considered to have created useless Egyptian pyramids. The mathematics used to build the Roman Colosseum was instrumental in creating the epitome of Greek artistic culture. However, its innate neurological disease was that the Colosseum, as an artistic expression, was used to excite the populace with acts of organized sadistic behaviour. The Nazi regime associated mathematical genius with exactly the same artistic concept, using the famous Greek discus thrower statue as a symbol associated with the bringing about of World War II.

Immanuel Kant was a Founding Father of the ethical basis of the electromagnetic Golden Age of Danish Science. The antidote begins to emerge from his research into locating the electromagnetic spiritual artistic ethic sought for by Plato. Kant, along with his contemporary, Emmanuel Levinas, concluded that the artistic spiritual element that Plato sought, belonged to an infinite, ethical, universal, Godlike purpose. Both Kant and Levinas quite specifically referred to this as an evolving emotional asymmetrical electromagnetic field existing within the creative artistic mind.

History's greatest mathematician, Georg Cantor's mathematics now underpins most of modern science, except for one fundamental concept, for which he became history's most vilified mathematician. From his research into ancient Greek science he considered that his infinite mathematics provided access to God's perpetual paradise. He published his conviction that the modern scientific mind was inhabited by a "myopic fear of infinity" that denied this ethical purpose. Both the Church and famous mathematicians of his day so savagely attacked him he was admitted to hospital, where he later died of starvation. However, Cantor had one supporter, the mathematician, David Hilbert, who, whilst working with Albert Einstein, provided the necessary electromagnetic evidence that allowed the antidote to the global disinformation epidemic to be discovered. a high resolution picture of the human cell poised to divide has been identified as being an infinite fractal mathematical expression. Epidemiologists attempting to find an antidote to the global dysfunctional information epidemic realized that Cantorian mathematical sensibility must, in some way, be involved with the healthy living process. Hilbert's biological asymmetrical electromagnetic field during the transfer of healthy information to the replica cell, will not allow dysfunctional information from gaining access to it. As this demonstrated Cantor's infinite mathematics as part of the living process, the epidemiologists, infected by a neurological denial of this, were unable to grasp its true significance.

In 2016 the Australian antidote discovery was presented to the pubic in Italy and Russia by

Italian quantum biologists and Quantum Art International, which had shared in its relevant research since 2010. At the Russian presentation it was awarded a first prize by the World Fund for Arts. In 2017 the World Fund for Arts, under the auspices of the Russian Government, laid the foundations for further Science-Art Research. If critical international debate eventuates from that initiative, then a sustainable political science should emerge to instigate the development of a future Science-Art technology.

The nature of future technology utilising the antidote became obvious from the writings of the mathematician and electrical engineer, Charles Proteus Steinmetz. He invented the asymmetrical electromagnetic alternating current motor, the fundamental basis of the electric power industry in the United States of America. Steinmetz wrote that instead of this physical technology, a far greater one was apparent in the form of an asymmetrical electromagnetic "spiritual" technology. Steinmetz had published works about the spiritual atomic science of ancient Greece.

Salvador Dali's eccentric and flamboyant criticisms of modern science entered the world of simple technological genius when it led to his conviction that paintings contained hidden ethical stereoscopic 3D messages. Dali actually wrote ï»¿"The discovery of invisible images certainly lies within my destiny". Every nuance within his struggle to come to terms with that emotional conviction warrants painstaking investigation by neurological scientists familiar with Guy Deutscher's revival of 19th Century linguistic colour perception theory. Deutscher's 2012 book of the year entitled 'Through the Language Glass' revised the 19th Century linguistic colour perception theories of Wolfgang von Goethe establishing a new neurological science.

Epidemiologists need to become acquainted with Dali's stereoscopic intuitions, constituting an evolutionary step towards the neurological visualization of reality, belonging to the world of the time crystal.

The Science-Art theories of Salvador Dali have been linked to his criticisms of the writings of some of the great scientific minds of the 19th and 20th Centuries. His investigations into political ideologies can be seen as a practical colour laboratory experimenting with Goethe's Science of Colour. Dali's artistic language about his feelings about art fused Freudian terminology into his own emotional feelings about the philosophy of science. Dali's artistic stereoscopic theories were associated with Immanuel Kant's electromagnetic theories about creative art and the existence of an infinite universal ethic inhabiting the creative mind.

The paper titled 'The Neural Sources of Salvador Dali's Ambiguity' by Semir Zeki, University College London, explores the complex functioning of Dali's mind concerning electromagnetic colour perception activity. Dali's experimental use of two asymmetrical paintings to pursue Kant's description of an evolving spiritual ethical asymmetrical electromagnetic field within the artistic creative mind has now been greatly developed. Australian Science-Artists discovered how to make Dali's invisible stereoscopic inner vision much more dramatically visible to the public.

In 2002 asymmetrical electromagnetic stereoscopic glasses were patented. By viewing single paintings through those glasses, the evolutionary process of Dali's artistic theories became undeniably apparent. The Australian research became so advanced that the visibility of 3D images apparently moving within individual paintings delivered aspects of 'Mind over Colour Torque Forces', of interest to engineers. They saw it as being contrary to the 'Colour over Mind' torque forces emanating from unethical poker-machine technology. Such concepts surely belong more to Charles Proteus Steinmetz's far superior asymmetrical electromagnetic spiritual technology than the one ordained by our prevailing dysfunctional thermodynamic culture.

Dali's stereoscopic art exhibitions throughout the world belong to a multi-million dollar business enterprise. If a new artistic presentation of his genius comes into existence for the general public then this will be the financial catalyst needed to usher in a multi-billion dollar human survival technology.

In 1979, the Science-Unit of Australian National Television, in its eight part scientific documentary series called 'The Scientists - Profiles of Discovery', predicted that this would happen. It dedicated one of the documentaries to the Australian Science-Art seashell discoveries, referring to it as "The Catalyst".

Crystal Meth - The Dance Of Death

We live in a society where faster is better. From instant noodles to fast food, high-speed computers to rapid transit, speed has become an important part of our culture.

Physically, many find it hard to keep up to our modern, frenetic pace. So they take over-the-counter pep pills, down loads of caffeinated colas or drink triple Mocha Lattés with giga-jolts of caffeine.

When these no longer work, some turn to more effective stimulant drugs. Why not, they're fast and they're potent, right? Yes, but they're also unsafe. They are a complex group of chemicals with one thing in common: the ability to wreck your life.

Ironically named speed, methamphetamine gives many the added energy they crave. Not only are more people using it, they're using the most potent and hyper-charged form: crystal meth. This drug, as cheap as it is toxic, has become the remedy of choice for a new generation of speed chasers.a 2004 Canadian Addiction Survey measured the use of speed in Canadians aged 15 and older. Results show that 6.4% of respondents reported using methamphetamines at least once in their life.

Another survey involving four B.C. school districts showed that up to 8% of students in grades 6-12 report having tried crystal meth in the 2005 school year.

Combined, these might not be earth-shattering statistics, but experts state that 90 percent of users are addicted after the first hit. Even one use of crystal meth can cause immediate, lasting physical and mental damage.

Still, such advice deters few. They smoke it, snort it, pop it or shoot it. Yet many don't understand what's in it. The folks who cook their meth aren't exactly government approved pharmacists. They are more likely to be sleazy individuals huddled over a bathtub mixing their poisonous brew in filthy conditions.

Lethal ingredients

An August 2004 CBC News article stated that clandestine labs have been found in homes, garages, motel rooms and even vehicles in middle class neighbourhoods. Meth can be manufactured in a short period of time, with a modest amount of materials. Basic ingredients from chemicals, solvents and equipment can be purchased in many stores.

Unlike legal drugs, the illicit type has no quality control, so users can never be sure of strength or purity. Ingredients vary in combination and are never exactly the same, says the Canadian Aids Society. Ephedrine (from over-the counter cold medicine), Drano, battery acid, insecticides, solvents, anhydrous ammonia, paint thinner and muriatic acid are among the mix.

These toxic substances form what some have described as a volatile mix of laundry detergent and lighter fluid. All that matters little because both those who use it, and those who manufacture it have a relationship. One party gets high and the other gets rich. Police say an investment of about $150 can yield up to $10,000 worth of the drug.

The attraction

Imagine a euphoric flood coursing through your body; an intensely super focused outlook, and infinite enthusiasm; making everything a riveting experience. That's the appeal of this drug to many partiers, or those seeking long term energy for mundane tasks.a 2005 New Yorker article stated that methamphetamine is a mood elevator, and is known to induce bursts of euphoria, increase alertness, and reduce fatigue. In slightly less concentrated forms, the drug has been used by truckers trying to drive through the night, by workers struggling to finish an extra shift, and by people seeking to lose weight.

It's not costly either. One can obtain amounts as small as one tenth of a gram, known as a point, for as little as five dollars. This is enough to give the user an intense high for up to 24 hours.

Considered trendy and popular as a club drug, meth has a strong presence in dance clubs, parties and raves. It provides enormous energy to keep gyrating all night to the pounding rhythms of the dance floor. It makes one feel full of life, powerful and sexual, shifting the libido into overdrive.

The risks

Crystal Meth is more toxic than crack and more addictive than heroin, and it literally fries your brain cells, say experts. If smoked or injected, the user experiences a powerful high called a flash. The first rush is always the most intense and chasing that initial feeling causes dependence quickly. More of the drug and higher doses are needed as the addiction progresses.

Such speed runs, over days and weeks, give little rest to body or mind. Typically, during this stage, the abuser has not slept from between three to fourteen days. At the end of the high, the user undergoes tweaking; feeling miserable, and uncomfortable, as well as possibly violent.

Chronic behavioural problems such as social isolation and withdrawal are compounded by extreme depression and suicidal ideation. According to the San Francisco Aids Foundation, the long term effects of methamphetamine use are horrendous.

The sores often seen on the bodies of users are from picking at the skin, due to the feeling of bugs crawling underneath. The obsession to dig or gouge them out is incessant. Some will use knives, glass, pins or needles to pick away for up to ten hours or more. Even when it becomes apparent that no bugs are there, the urge remains. The skin becomes infected and is extremely nasty looking.

Then there's the danger of meth teeth, the result of poor oral hygiene by users. Brittle and cracked teeth, gum infections, disease, and general decay are rampant among users. Unless seen, it is hard to comprehend the total dental destruction of long term abusers. Teeth are so brittle, that even eating ice cream may cause them to fall out. a November 2005 Washington Post article states that the drug causes lasting changes in brain chemistry, particularly in the neurotransmitter systems. Notably, the churning out of massive amounts of dopamine seems to affect cognitive abilities such as memory, judgment, reasoning, and verbal skills.

Dr. Paul Thompson, an expert on brain mapping at the University of California, Los Angeles, proved massive brain damage using high-resolution M.R.I. studies on people addicted for up to ten years.

Quoted in a 2004 New York Times article, he said he expected some brain changes but didn't expect so much tissue to be destroyed.

The image, published in the June 30 issue of The Journal of Neuroscience, shows the brain's surface and deeper limbic system, which is involved in drug cravings, mood and emotion, lost 11 percent of its tissue.

The hippocampus, the part of the brain that deals with memory also lost 8 percent of its tissue. The article states that this is comparable to brain deficits in early Alzheimer's cases. Heavy users can experience psychotic episodes, characterized by paranoia and auditory and visual hallucinations, according to Prevention Source BC.

The long-term physical toll may also include vitamin and mineral deficiencies, lowered resistance to disease, and organ damage, particularly to the lungs, liver, and kidneys. The vicious cycle also may damage blood vessels in the brain, which can cause strokes, or lead the heart to beat irregularly. Cardiovascular collapse and death have been known to happen.

Quitting is not easy

It's about as easy to quit crystal meth as trying to stop a runaway train. The San Francisco Aids Foundation states that after stopping the drug, the user experiences a profound numbness and depression, as the body no longer stimulates enough to experience pleasure. This can become so overpowering, suicidal thoughts may be considered to ease the pain.

Crashing often entails severe lack of energy, and a massive lack of motivation to perform normal tasks. The day after coming down, the user feels sick, depressed, guilty, ashamed and angry. He wants to quit, but the cravings are unnaturally strong. The only thing that takes them away is more crystal meth. But soon the high becomes disappointing; euphoria turns to numbness, focus is replaced by confusion, and productivity disappears.

According to a former addict, "It's more than something that you become addicted to. It becomes your whole reason for living. You just want it so much that you'd give anything for it. You can't describe it, unless you've seen it. You can't explain it, unless you've done it. You can't imagine it, unless you've been there. Then, it never goes away."

Recovery

If you're a junkie, you have to hit rock bottom before you can climb back up. Experts say that crystal meth is one of the most addictive street drugs and one of the hardest to treat. The relapse rate of 92 per cent is worse than cocaine. In

Canada, provincial health insurance and government recovery programs provide help and assistance for the addict to recover.

But the withdrawal symptoms, especially depression and physical agony, cause many to drop out. The simplest and most effective strategy is not to get addicted. This is not an easy sell for young people, but can be effectively illustrated by those who have experienced an addiction. The struggles of peers are starkly more powerful than simple messages quoting the dangers.

The overall message to people is that crystal meth wrecks lives; abuses health, and destroys families. Ultimately, the need for speed kills. And what it doesn't kill, it burns out. Get the message?

Crystal Experiments You Can Share With Your Kids

Suppose we have a drop of water. If we look at it very closely, we'll see a drop of water, nice and smooth. If you grab your microscope and magnify it roughly 2,000 times (the drop is now 40 feet across, the size of a large classroom) and look very closely, we'll still see relatively smooth water, but there are wiggly things floating around (paramecia). We could stop here and study these interesting little critters, but then, we'd side-track ourselves into biology. So let's focus more on the water.

Let's magnify the water 2,000 times again, so it's roughly 15 miles across. When we look at it very closely now, we see what looks like a teeming mob of Super Bowl fans making their way to the nearest exit - lots and lots of movement, but it's still fuzzy and hard to make out. Now we'll magnify it another 250 times (for a total magnification of roughly 1 billion times), and we'll see two kinds of "blobs" - hydrogen atoms and oxygen atoms arranged in a little group like Mickey Mouse. Each little group of these atoms is called a molecule.

This picture on the right is idealized in a few ways, but most importantly, it doesn't move on the page, whereas the real molecule wiggles and jiggles as we watch it magnified 1 billion times. Another way this picture is not quite right is that the atoms are really stuck together like glue, much the same way magnets attract each other. But unlike magnets, if you squeeze these atoms together too hard, they repel.

The jiggling motion is what we call heat. When we increase the temperature (say, water over a hot stove), the jiggles increase and the volume between the atoms increase.

Suppose now we decrease the temperature of our drop of water, and we find the jiggling motion decreases, and the attractive forces between the atoms takes over and at very low temperatures, the atoms lock together into a new pattern called ice. The interesting thing is that there is a place for every atom in its solid form (crystalline array). Water is one of the only molecules that expands when solidified. The crystal pattern of ice is shown (right) - it has many holes in it. This open structure collapses when the atoms jiggle hard enough to shake themselves loose (melting) and rush to fill in the gaps as the temperature (and jiggling) increases.

How big is an atom? If an orange is magnified to the size of the earth, the size of the atoms in the orange are approximately the size of the original orange.

Crystals are made by either solidifying (think about the ice crystals in your freezer), or by "growing" them (as in the homschool science activities we're about to start). Let's find out more about how to grow (or "farm") your own crystals.

When making crystals, there is a very special kind of solution to make. It's called a "super saturated solid solution". What does that mean? Here's an example: If you constantly add salt by the spoonful to a cup of water, you'll reach a point where the salt doesn't disappear (dissolve) anymore and forms a lump at the bottom of the glass.

The point at which it begins to form a lump is just past the point of being a saturated solution. If you heat up the saltwater, the lump disappears. You can now add more and more salt, until it can't take anymore salt (you'll see another lump starting to form at the bottom). This is now a super saturated solid solution. Mix in a bit of water to make the lump disappear. Your solution is ready for making crystals. But how?

If you add something for the crystals to cling to, like a rock or a stick, crystals can now grow. If you "seed" the object (coat it with the stuff you formed the solution with, like salt or sugar), they will start forming faster.

TIP for Speedy Crystals: If you keep the solution in a warm place, crystals may grow faster. Use the highest place in your house, a heating pad, or enclosed box with a lit light bulb (such as an overnight ride in the oven).

If you have too much salt (or other solid) mixed in, your solution will crystallize all at the same time and you'll get a huge rock that you can't pull out of the jar. If you have too little salt, then you'll wait forever for crystals to grow. Finding the right amount to mix in takes time and patience.

Geodes A geode is a crystallized mineral deposit, and are usually very dull and ordinary-looking on the outside, until you crack them open! An eggshell is going to be used to simulate a gas bubble found in flowing lava. By dissolving alum in water (real life uses minerals dissolved in ground water) and placing it into your eggshell (in real life, it's a gas bubble pocket), you will be left with a geode. (Note: these crystals are not for eating, just looking.)

Making the Geode Make sure your eggshells are clean. Fill a small cup with warm water and dissolve as much alum in the water as you can to make a saturated solution (meaning that if you add any more alum, it will only fall to the bottom and not dissolve). Fill the eggshells with the solution and set aside. Observe as the solution evaporates over the next few days. When the solution has completely evaporated, you will have a homemade geode. If no crystals formed, then you had too much water and not enough alum in your solution.

Gemstones Fill a clean glass jar with saturated solution made above and leave it for two days. Strain it and save the water for later. Keep the crystals!

String Crystals Fill another glass jar with spare saturated solution, and suspend a crystal (from experiment above) with string from the jar lid. Lower it into the solution and wait several days. (Seed the string for quicker growth.)

Rock Candy We're going to take advantage of the process of crystallization to make candy. You are going to make a super saturated solution of sugar and use it to grow your own homemade sugar candy crystals. A super saturated solution is one that has as much sugar dissolved in the water as possible. (If we didn't heat the water, we'd wind up with only a saturated solution.)

Making Rock Candy Boil three cups of water in a large pot on the stove. Add eight cups of sugar, one cup at a time, slowly stirring as you go. The liquid should be thick and yellowish. Turn off the heat and let it sit for four hours (or until the temperature is below 120 degrees F). Pour the sugar water solution into clean glass jars and add a couple drops of food coloring (for colored crystals). Tie a string to a skewer, resting the skewer horizontally across the jar mouth.

Jelly Crystals This water jelly crystal (found in the gardening section of your hardware store, usually called "Soil Moist") will grow over 300 times its own size when hydrated (adding water). Fill each cup half full of water. Add a few drops of food coloring and stir. Add a handful of crystals and let stand 20 minutes. Squish them with your hands! Combine several different colors (in layers) in a empty water bottle and watch the colors melt into each other (try layering blue, yellow, and red and watch orange and green appear out of nowhere!) Make a huge rainbow wand using a plastic fluorescent tube casing (from the hardware store - they come in 4 to 8' sections!) with stoppers glued to the ends. To reuse crystals, lay on a paper towel and let dry (they may stain beneath the towel, so add a layer of foil) over a few days.

Salt Stalactites Make a saturated solution from warm water and Epsom salts. (Add enough salt so that if you add more, it will not dissolve further.) Fill two empty glass jars with the salt solution. Space the jars a foot apart on a layer of foil or on a cookie sheet. Suspend a piece of yarn or string from one jar to the other. Wait impatiently for about three days. A stalactite should form from the middle of the string!

Healing Gemstones & Crystals - Inspiring Wellness And Balance

Throughout the centuries, holistic healers have utilized the spiritual and healing properties found in gemstones and crystals. Whether it be to bring about the balance or wellness for themselves and their clients, or as a means of healing ones chakras. However, healing gemstones aren't just for holistic healers anymore! Many people are beginning to take the power of gemstones within their own hands. But, how do you find the crystals or gemstones that will be appropriate for you?

Finding the appropriate gemstones for your needs might be difficult, however once you begin to understand their history and power; it will be easy to select the right ones. The primary use of gemstones and crystals throughout history has been for healing or spiritual purposes. However, during these times the gems were thought to be rare. Causing them to be available for a select few. Luckily, today they are more readily accessible to everyone who wants them.

There are a few people who are skeptical on the powers of gemstones. However the powers of gemstones and crystals, are even recognized by modern science. You may not know that they are utilized in watches, lasers, computers, and even in potencies. Regardless of this backing of science, they still have yet to prove or dis-prove their ability to promote physical healing in the body.

Gems and crystals all have magnetic powers in varying degrees. Of which many are extremely beneficial for the use of healing on the human form. They are known to emit small vibrations and frequencies, that have a strong potential to affect our being. In many different religions and practices, gems are used for healing, transforming, attuning, and balancing the body mind and soul. Used frequently to activate our own personal abilities to sooth, comfort, heal, and balance ones self in many different aspects.

However, despite the abilities of gemstones; many people still have yet to experience the healing ways of gemstones and crystals. Some of the first steps you will need to know about gems, is how to cleanse them of any past energies.

The gem in question should be cleaned either by leaving them under running water for six to eight hours. Or can also be buried in the earth overnight (rinsing them off afterward of course!). otherwise you can place them over the flame of a candle until it melts. Once you have cleaned your gemstone, it should be placed in direct sunlight for purification; as it is a wonderful source of energy.

Remember, you should wear your stones. They are of little use to you when sitting in a jewelry box. Having a healing gemstone with you at all times, can help to heal both your body mind and spirit; with little to no effort on your part. Simply being in tune with the stone, and allowing it to work it's energy over your body is enough.

Once you have decided to embark on the quest for knowledge about healing gemstones, you will need to have an open mind and heart. There are many different theories out there about why and how the healing powers of gemstones work; however some can become convoluted and jaded with time. Simply believe in the stones, and allow the energy to work it's own kind of magic.

Whether you are a newcomer to the world of healing stones, or an old soul simply looking for information on a possible new stone. There are many different gemstones or crystals to choose from. Some of the most popular, and not-so well known stones and their abilities are.

- Rose Quarts is one of the most popular gemstones use for healing. It is known for it's gentle healing energies, used mostly for it's heart-healing possibilities. It is used to strengthen the heart from physical ailments, all the way to a cure for emotional heartbreak. It is also used as a gift for those who needs to learn how to love themselves.

- Fluorite: another popular stone among the gemstone community. While available in many different colors, it is a stone that can help to guard someone against negativity. In short, this stone will absorb any negative energy near-by and help to keep it at bay. Remember, with stones that are known to absorb negative energies, you will need to cleanse them at least once a week.

- Lapis: a top-dog in the world of gemstones. It is said to help unlock mysteries. Used commonly to help it's wearer through confusion and emotional blocks.

- Hematite: A grounding stone that is used by many. It's silver-grey metallic coloration unmistakable for any other gemstone. It is often used as a grounding tool for those who wish to avoid worldly tasks or events by utilizing out of body flight.

- Amethyst: this beautiful purple stone is often times associated with spiritual healing. It is known to help attune its wearer to a higher awareness and knowing.

- Jade: Utilized to teach acceptance through it's calming energy. It is used to help someone become less critical of themselves and others.

- Turquoise: while used simply for it's beauty in jewelry. It is a stone that can be used for it's teaching powers. It is a stone that is frequently used to aid in meditation or dream visions.

- Kyanite: is used by experienced gemstone healers. It is best utilized by wearing it close to the throat chakra. It is used as a focus to facilitate channeling and opening communication centers. Unlike so many other gemstones, this brilliant stone can and will cleanse itself of negative energies.

- Citrine: another front-runner in the world of gemstones. It is a beautiful yellow stone, that will help to manifest your goals. It can help to attract abundance and personal power.

- Obsidian: Is used once more as a grounding or protective agent. It is known to help bring forth the opportunity of change, serenity, and clarity.

- Amazonite: A gemstone that is used to help improve self worth.

- Amber: Used to lift the heaviness of burden. Which will allow happiness a means to enter your life once more.

- Apatite: Another stone that is frequently used to open up communication in your world. It is used when there has been a misunderstanding, and can help to calm any anxiety that has stemmed from a fight.

- Green Aventurine: Is used for physical healing. It is worn over the ailing part of the body.

- Blue Aventurine: Is used to improve circulation of blood.

- Coral: Is used as a foundation for your emotions.

- Diamond: It's not just a girl's best friend guys! It is used to help with personal clarity.

- Emerald: is used for physical and emotional healing. It is by far one of the strongest healing gemstones that have been found to date.

- Carnelian: Used as balance and a method to aid in creativity and the mental process.

- Grey Moonstone: Utilized as a focus for others stones, enabling you their energies as well as the moonstone's energy.

- Moss Agate: Used to get in touch with mother nature herself, also used as a grounding stone in meditation.

- Mexican Onyx: Is used to help insomnia and other sleeping disorders.

- Black opal: This stone will help to focus your body soul and mind.

- Ruby: Often times associated with love and romance. It is used to open up the heart-chakra to allow the feeling of love in.

- Sapphire: A beautiful stone that is known to help mental clarity.

Unfortunately, there are too many stones available to list them all in a small series of articles. To enlighten yourself further on the powers of healing gemstones, and what gems are used for; you may look into purchasing a healing gemstone book. They will help you to further your knowledge of healing gemstones. Which, as you might have already learned is an important step in utilizing their healing powers.

Crystal And Indigo Energies

The New Children (aka Indigo, Crystal, Rainbow, Star Children) are everywhere. They are highly evolved souls incarnating now to help ascend humanity into unity consciousness.

Anyone interested enough to be reading this probably has a role in assisting the New Children in some way - even just through your awareness and appreciation of them.

As we move towards 2012 and beyond, the New Children are becoming even more consciously aware of their true selves and of their mission. The early-wavers have worked hard and in very difficult challenges to break down old energies enough to allow the new-wavers in.

Many of the early-wavers have been the ones labelled with ADHD and ADD or have had difficult childhoods and adolescences as they

143

have broken down old educational, familial and societal structures.

New Children are still human

The New Children are very special and precious, but they usually look and act like 'normal' children for the most part. But we have become accustomed to these children gradually and often believe their more assertive, loving, sensitive, creative, telepathic, disruptive and/or wise natures are just a product of a new generation.

However, I'd bet that if we went back to our parents or grandparents generation, and even our own childhoods and hung out with kids for a while, the contrast would be easy to see.

It is so important to know that these children still act like children - they cry, whinge, fight, tantrum, fail, get scared, and love the usual kids games and toys.

They are in the human experience too so they are working within the matrix of the collective human energy and have lower egos. If you feel your child is of the New Children, but doubted it because they seemed too 'normal' then please remember this.

Not many of them are doing things that are obviously magical or spiritual. Although they are telepathic, psychic and have abilities to do things like levitate, practice telekinesis and even teleport, we don't usually see much or any evidence of it in day to day life.

You may see them waving their fingers or hands around, or do things like bend their forehead to yours, as they shift energy and do their healing work. A lot of their work is done during the sleep state.

Some of them are guardians and holders of the light that is flooding the Earth now to ensure that it 'sticks'.

Highly sensitive to energies

They are all sensitive and this means that they can get easily overwhelmed. Because they are so empathic, their own energy soaks up the energies around them and this can make them behave in very agitated, erratic and hyper ways as they struggle to cope with the overwhelm.

This can turn into a difficult cycle where their behaviour gets them labelled as 'difficult', when really they just need to get back into their own balanced energy.

Instead of acting out, other children may retreat from any conflict and turn the other cheek whilst absorbing negativity and then trying to transmute it all.

Either way these sensitive children need protection from negativity and tools to help them balance their energies. Just teaching them to ask themselves, 'Is this energy mine?' is very useful.

Help them stay balanced

It is important that parents realise they are guardians of very special souls who find it difficult to be in dense energies. If they are immersed for too long in heavy energies, they can forget their true selves and lose their path, or at least go off on an unpleasant and disruptive tangent.

This is the risk that these courageous souls take in incarnating in a density they are un-used to, so anything their guardians can do to help them stay balanced and in touch with their true selves is vital.

Lots of time outdoors in nature, swimming, clean foods and water, avoiding the rigid adherence to strict routines and disciplines, more flexible educational structures and of course lots of love help them keep balanced.

Unique gifts and qualities

Each soul has its own purpose, so each child reflects different qualities. Some are very outgoing, assertive (bossy even) and energetic because that will best serve them in their purpose. Some are quiet and relatively inactive because that might serve them in their role. Some are intellectually gifted, some are highly creative. There is no norm for the New Child.

As parents and caretakers of these souls we need to be aware and supportive of their true tendencies and passions.

Most of all they need love. This is why they search for validation and acceptance from the world and will do everything they can to ensure that they get it. If they don't, they can react by withdrawing their energy, themselves and their love.

We must be aware of projecting our desires and fears on to them. If a child from a family with an intensely academic and professional focus seems to rebel and want to be a garbo or a gardener, s/he may be serving the purpose of breaking an old matrix pattern of rigidity and inauthenticity. And maybe just following their passions. Every time an old and unhelpful system is broken down it serves the whole.

It's weird to label these children but just look at it as a way to understand them more:

Indigo - these are the first-wavers of the New Children and are known as systems busters or spiritual warriors. They started coming in as early as the 1940s, with large numbers coming in the 1960s and 70s. We now have quite a number of Indigo adults around. a huge influx of souls carrying indigo energies arrived in the 1990s, and more so since 2000.

Some of these kids have given us the ADHD and ADD phenomenon - they are busting up crusty old systems of education and society that were based on control and limitation. Doreen Virtue reckons ADHD should stand for Attention Dialed into a Higher Dimension. These kids cannot and will not be controlled with inauthentic power. They respond only to real respect and love.

They are very brave souls and have faced great difficulties in their roles. They have often experienced a lot of anguish and conflict in being so sensitive and in busting up the old, and in some cases being put on drugs like Ritalin to try to control them.

Their families, teachers and supporters also deserve our appreciation for their invaluable role in this change. It has been hard for them too and they have often not known how to deal with the indigo energies.

There has been a phenomenon of suicides by some indigos who have become too overwhelmed with life. There have also been some who have really gone off the rails and committed very violent acts.

The light side of these dark acts has been in the breaking down of systems that were not working and the raising of awareness of how children and teenagers are educated and treated.

Crystal - the crystal or 'Christed' energy is heart-based. Children carry different levels of indigo and crystal energies, with some being very indigo and some very crystal, but many carry both.

Crystal energies are very loving and compassionate...but they can also be very feisty and angry. They are in a human experience after all.

Their very loving natures are what shines through most, especially when they are balanced and in pleasant surroundings. They often love talk of hearts, angels and love, and are affectionate and loving in a delightfully free and natural way.

Children with a lot of crystalline energy are more likely to withdraw themselves from day to day life if they are overwhelmed, as opposed to indigo energies which are more likely to act out. The surge in autism and Asperger's is linked to crystal children who are living in a very different dimension a lot of the time.

Many crystals are slow to talk because they are so telepathic they don't see a need for it.

They may think in such different and creative ways that are not aligned with traditional 'old school' education methods. More flexible approaches to education are so important for these and other New Children because they will not respond well to rigid and fixed regimes.

It is lovely to acknowledge the New Children, either verbally or telepathically. Thank them for coming to Earth and for what they are doing here. Acknowledge that you know they are a highly evolved soul in a little human body and that you appreciate them. It is a big love-fest and brings much tenderness, love and appreciation between you.

Indigo/Crystal Phenomena

There are many things that we can do to help these new breed of children, but the most important thing to know is that the Indigo/Crystal phenomenon is the next big step in our human evolution. We all are, in some way or another, becoming more like the Indigo and Crystal people. The more one chooses to consciously work towards change, the faster the results will be for that individual. This new breed of children (which truly isn't all that new, just massive amounts now) have come to show us the way as we have forgotten. They are our mirrors. Which simply means they mirror what is inside of us, all that needs to change in order to evolve or raise our consciousness. They have come here to help change the vibrations of our lives and to create peace, balance and harmony.

Therefore, the Indigos have emerged to knock down the old outdated systems! They are warriors and they are on a mission! They create chaos everywhere they go. They can sense dishonesty a mile away and are unable to conform to dysfunctional situations within their homes, schools and work places. Gone are the days of threatening "wait till your father gets home," or "you'll be suspended," the Indigos don't care! They have inner-lie detectors and will not be manipulated nor fall for hidden agendas. They are very head strong and do not like to be told what to do, nor do they want to do it your way. If we do not break out of our old control habits, threat habits or any other destructive behaviour, they will show us that we must learn new methods in order for peace to prevail! This is done through heart connections, with love. They simply do not have the ability to disassociate from their feelings and pretend that everything is okay. They respond the best to all situations when they are treated like a respected adult. If we are acting childish in a manipulating, hurtful way, they will mirror back to us our own behaviour. This causes more frustration within ourself than it does within them! Their goal is for US to change, not them. Their horns toot "Treat others as you would want to be treated!" They are not shy in letting you know exactly what they need. Watch them. They have no hidden agenda. They are our teachers!

The Indigos are creating chaos with the end result being a peaceful, loving world. Many, but not all Indigos are labeled by the medical world as Attention Deficit/Hyperactivity Disorder or more commonly known as ADD/ADHD because they can't be still, they can't focus, they bore easily, they are impulsive and they do things super fast. Giving them medication is not the answer! That is once again a control factor not to mention all the detrimental health problems including death that occurs from these types of medications. Indigo and Crystal children are extremely intelligent and need their minds stimulated with things they enjoy to do. They have amazing memories and are gifted souls with an evolved consciousness. They need to be taught in a different way, through subjects they love that stimulate their whole beings! We are moving beyond the mind and into the heart. These Indigo children will not conform to the old ritual text book teachings. This system is old and needs to be replaced. They are trying to show the teachers of the school systems that they need a new way of learning. This is beginning to happen.

How can you tell if you are an Indigo? A good way to "test" yourself is to answer the following:

Y Are you always searching for your greater purpose in life but feel like the world isn't set up for your kind?

Y Do you feel wise beyond your years?

Y Do you have trouble conforming to the ways of society? Y Do you feel out of place in today's world?

Y Do you perceive the world very differently than most people around you?

Y Do you have strong intuition about certain things that most others do not?

Y Do you often feel misunderstood when you try to talk to people about what's real?

Y Do you feel like you were born to accomplish a special mission in life? Y Do you feel isolated and alone in your beliefs?

Y Misunderstood by family? Perhaps the black sheep of the family?

Y Do you feel anti-social unless you are with people of like mind? Y Are you emotionally sensitive?

Y Did you have a difficult childhood?

Y Do you often feel disempowered by too much authority?

If you can answer yes to these questions, then you are most likely an Indigo. If you want outside validation than you may want to find a person who has honed the gift of clairvoyance, the gift of seeing what most people do not. The clairvoyant person while looking at you or tuning into your energy field, will be able to tell if you are Indigo or not by the colour of your aura which is the invisible energy field surrounding your physical body. You can also have an aura photo taken to see for yourself your own colours.

So what can I do to help my child?

Through my own experience, I have learnt that it is extremely important to have harmonious energy within our environments, to stay grounded and keep shielded. I believe if this small piece of advice hit mainstream schools it would make a huge difference in all the kids temperaments! I am an Indigo/Crystal and a single mom or four Indigo/Crystal children and know first hand that if the energy within our home is 'off' the children are wild! They will be much more aggressive towards one another, more fighting, crying and very restless. They have more temper tantrums and mood swings and refuse any kind of authority! When the home is energetically balanced, they are much more relaxed, calm, gentle and peaceful. Ahh, normal kids!

Leaving our energetically balanced, sacred space to go out into public places, un-protected is a living nightmare! The change within my children's temperament is like watching Jekyll and Hyde! Onlookers or unaware people would perceive this to be children that are wild or have had way too much sugar or more commonly "the mother has no control." My oldest child especially is affected. He's ten and has been diagnosed as 'ADHD.' When we finally get back inside our vehicle and start the drive home, they all will have begun to calm down. (I have adjusted the energy of our vehicle to be harmonious as well.) Not long after we have entered our house, usually they have begun to 'crash'. It's similar to a sugar high, they are at their peak of explosion in public because of the denser energies and when they get back into their own frequency they start to burn out because of the chaos their bodies have experienced! Talk about detrimental to their health. I have provided a list of things below that work wonderfully well for us in creating our sacred environment and other things to empower my Indigo/Crystal Kids.

BREATHE! Breathing moves energy. When they are frustrated, scared, hyper, etc. ask them to Stop and Breathe deeply. Inhale through the nose and exhale through the mouth. Tell them to really exert the out blow, like blowing out your anger! Make it fun and do it with them.

Smudge your home to help clear the distracting vibrations. This needs to be done immediately after a blow up of any sort and on a regular basis. Make it part of your house cleaning routine! I smudge a lot, sometimes daily depending upon what the kids have picked up from school. This truly makes an amazing difference!

Staying 'Grounded' is very important. There are many methods of how this is done. I personally like something that is fast and easy to do. Intention and visualizing are quick easy methods and can be done in a second at anytime, without anyone even noticing! The first thing I do is ask Gaia (Mother Earth) her permission for my grounding cord to enter the core of her being. Then I visualize a clear cord or clear rope coming from my root chakra (tail bone area) and entering Gaia. It grows in length, and continues to grow until it has been fully anchored into the core of Gaia. This grounding cord releases negative energy and also brings in positive energy. Set your intention to send all the negative energy down this cord, physically exhale, releasing it into Gaia. After the negative energy has all been released, with intention bring up the positive life-giving earth energy with a physical inhale. Thank Gaia and do not worry that this will hurt her, it doesn't! Have your kids make a monkey chain cord. It's the intention that works!

Staying 'Shielded' is also very important. Indigos and Crystals are extremely sensitive. Their highly tuned energy fields pick up negative emotions and environmental energy from their surroundings like a sponge which cause severe mood swings. Imagine being in a room where there are four depressed people, three angry people and the room itself has not been energetically cleared from all the emotional yuck for years! The Indigo unknowingly will pick up all this energy and take it on as their own! And people wonder why they are labeled as ADHD! Teach them to create and surround themselves with the "bubble of white light" protection every morning! This repels the negative energy around them but allows the positive energy to enter. The bubble would look like a soap bubble with them inside of it.

EXERCISE. It is important for exercise to remain a part of all of our lives, but this also helps the Indigo/Crystal Children to rid themselves of excess energy as their nervous systems are wired differently than others. Excellent exercise outlets to release what they are holding in their emotional, mental, physical and spiritual bodies are: Martial Arts, Yoga, Karate, Tai-Chi, Dance Classes, Running, Skipping, Gymnastics: Anything they love that gets them moving!

Bring nature indoors. Lots of beautiful plants, rocks, crystals, waterfalls, aquariums etc.a quiet space with no electrical equipment in the room. This is a room for them to just BE. Do whatever they love to do in their quiet time. Be it art work, read, puzzles, lego blocks, etc.

Nightly baths in sea salt. Be sure to drink extra water as this pulls toxins from the physical body and also clears negative energies from the energetic body.

[Put sea salt on their names with their permission. The salt pulls out all the negative energies that no longer serve them. Let this sit for 24 hours, then dump the salt into the toilet.

[The removal of all artificial scents is a must! Use only the highest quality oils and unscented beeswax candles.

[Play dolphin, orca, and angelic relaxing music. Screaming chaotic music is only going to disturb their energy.

[Keep all electrical stuff out of their bedrooms. They simply can't tolerate the very dangerous electromagnetic waves these devices send out. This will help them sleep deeply and peacefully.

[Be honest with them at all times with no manipulation about all things, toning it down to their age level. If you don't you will have a war on your hands!

[Reiki Energy Healing, Sound Healing, and other alternative healing methods are recommended for healing, balancing, rejuvenating and empowering not just Indigos but all of us!

We are moving into a wonderful new world where peace will reside! That's a beautiful thing.

Healing Benefits Of Crystals And Stones

Agate - This crystal will allow you self-confidence by stimulating your inner talents, releasing your creativity, and allowing you a greater capacity to think and analyze. As well as relieving tensions and fears, Agate will help you to excel in all aspects.

Amber - This powerful crystal will intake all negativity around you and replace it with positivity - these forces will allow the body to self-heal. For those who have suicidal feelings, Amber is also a very good Feng Shui cure for your depression.

Amethyst - This stone will create clarity of mind and more serene moods, therefore allowing your inner creativity and knowledge to flow. It is a very good Feng Shui cure for those who suffer from insomnia or constant nightmares, as it will stimulate the peace and tranquility of your thoughts.

Aquamarine - For those who have trouble expressing their feelings and speaking out loud, the Feng Shui benefits of this crystal will help you; by repressing your fears and relieving anxiety, you will form the self-confidence and perseverance to get through tough times. During tests or meditation is a good time to use Aquamarine.

Aventurine - This crystal is very useful in creating concentration and focus, allowing for quick decision-making and a better flow of creativity. In addition to this, your ability to lead others will be enhanced, and you will have a greater ability to overcome obstacles in your path.

Bloodstone - This magical stone, in addition to being a very good blood cleaner, has the potency to ward off evil spirits and repress negative intentions headed your way, protecting you from any danger.

Carnelian - For those who are seeking the tools to advance in life, this stone will enhance perseverance, confidence, creativity and leadership, allowing you to better analyze and understand situations around you.

Charoite - This stone is a potent Feng Shui cure for those who suffer from compulsions and obsessive actions. In addition to this, it will repress stress by removing any negative energy in your life and revitalizing your chi. Used Charoite will leave you relaxed and anxiety-free.

Clear Quartz - This beautiful crystal has a potent energy power which can transform energy in many ways. It will also defend you against those who wish to harm you and cause you pain.

Garnet - This stone is regarded as the stone of romance, passion and wellbeing. It will remove any depression and stress from your life, and enhance feelings of lust, sexuality and intimacy, allowing you to feel closer to your partner and happier in life.

Hematite - This crystal is highly regarded as a physical healer, due to its powers to rejuvenate the body's oxygen supply and improving circulation by inducing the absorption of iron by your red blood cells.

Jade - In ancient China, this stone has long-since been wanted for its abilities to both heal and protect. A symbol of the beautiful and pure of heart, this stone will also allow for mental clarity and a stronger flow of intelligence and creativity.

Jasper - For those who suffer from headaches, migraines and stress, this stone is the ideal Feng Shui cure; it will calm your mind and induce serenity, allowing you to release your anxiety and feel more at peace with your soul.

Lapis Lazuli - This crystal is a symbol of a high spirit, as it will heighten your sense of adventure and allow you to feel more in control of your own life. In addition to this, your fears will be repressed and you will see the world in a clearer sense.

Moonstone - This stone, mostly used as a Feng Shui cure for women, will solve many problems that they deal with; period cramps, stress during menopause, and obstacles with fertility. In addition to this, females who use the Moonstone will be enhancing their feminine qualities, stimulating inner intuition and becoming more outwardly attractive.

Obsidian - This stone is the perfect Feng Shui cure for those who suffer from low self-esteem and need a heightened confidence. In addition to this, it is the ideal defense against negative chi in your life, and will defend you from those with evil motives.

Onyx - For those who are recently got out of a tough relationship and are trying to move on, the Onyx stone is a good Feng Shui remedy to heal your heart. It will also keep negative energy and away from you, keeping your mindset positive and happy.

Peridot - This stone is widely used by those who are looking to overcome the past, allowing them to let go of grudges and old feelings. Your heart will be open and fresh, and there will be no more feelings of resentment, jealousy or rage.

Prehnite - This stone will ensure that you are ready for any situation that comes your way. It is also known as the stone of "unconditional love", and is able to fix any wounds or emotional problems. In addition to this, Prehnite will increase your intuition.

Rhodochrosite - In Feng Shui, this crystal is an icon of compassion and romance, and the constant giving in relationships. It is also used for people who suffer from depression and denial after tragedies, as well as to improve self-esteem and emotional issues.

Rose Quartz - Known as the "Love Stone", this beautiful item helps in all aspects of romance; helping singles seek their life partner, improving the quality of a long term relationship, and fixing those with broken hearts.

Ruby -A crystal which revitalizes a lust for life, this item provides happiness for those are seeking a greater passion and happiness in their ventures. It will allow you to reach your goals and attain your aspirations, as well as keep your wealth safe from theft or loss.

Rutilated Quartz - This stone has properties which heal depression, insomnia, guilt and sad feelings, replacing them with emotions of inspiration and romance. Because of this, Rutilated Quartz has the potency to revive relationships and create a refreshed sense of hope and creativity.

Sapphire - Known as the "wisdom stone", this crystal induces just that; a sense of mental clarity which removed all negative thoughts and allows you a new mindset. While normal Sapphire is said to release mental tension, blue Sapphire is known to enhance emotions of love.

Smoky Quartz - This crystal is a good Feng Shui remedy for those who suffer from laziness and lethargy. By eliminating electromagnetic smog, an electromagnetic field which has dangerous effects on some, it creates an environment for higher focus and common sense.

Sodalite - This stone allows people to discover their inner truths, and express these and stand by them no matter the situation. It is also a useful stone to eliminate any electromagnetic fields, especially those which are emitted by technology.

Tiger's Eye - Those who use the Tiger's Eye attain a new drive for life and strive for success. By enhancing your confidence, loyalty, power and positivity, this stone will enable you to take your passion and make it happen.

Turquoise - This beautiful crystal is used by many to revitalize their chi as well as to attain a sense of peace. Turquoise is also a Feng Shui cure for broken relationships, creating loyalty and hope. Use this stone to improve communication with those around you.

Watermelon Tourmaline - For those who are looking to find new love and be accepting of the relationship, using this stone will allow you the tolerance and patience to deal with your potential partner. In addition to this, you will love yourself more, and feel more joy and at peace.

Zoisite - This crystal is an effective Feng Shui remedy for those who suffer from lethargy and depression; it does this by removing negativity and providing positivity. In addition to this, you will attain higher concentration and creativity by using Zoisite.

How To Use A Crystal Ball

Step 1. Preparation

Most people find crystal ball gazing is easiest in a quiet, dimly lit room. Many people like to have candles burning. For some the reflections of the flames help to summon images - others find them a distraction. Burning incence is common and some people like to have soothing music playing gently in the background.The important thing to remember is that you are creating an atmosphere.

The important key when doing crystal ball gazing is that you must be relaxed and your mind must be clear. It is always best to perform a cleansing ritual followed by a protection ritual, and THEN begin your crystal ball work. Normally a cleansing ritual would be performed on night one. The next night you would perform a protection ritual on yourself and within the room you intend on performing the crystal ball gazing. On the third night you can then be well prepared to use your crystal ball. Even though these rituals are not necessity, it is always wise to do them for maximum safety and best results.

When performing any form of scrying or divination you are summoning forth forces from the spirit realm. Normally these forces are closed off from this plane we live in unless otherwise disturbed such as through specific rituals such as crystal ball gazing and scrying. When you perform divination these forces can either aid you in bringing forth images of the future or other events, or attack you.

Evil spirits and negative influences can use your crystal ball, scrying mirror, ouija board, or pendulum a link for them to step through into this world. They can also use it as a means to drain energy from you as well. This is why it is always best to ensure proper cleansing and protection is prepared before hand.

Step 2. The Crystal Ball Gazing Method

Place the crystal ball on a table in front of you. Many crystal balls you can buy come with their own stand. If you don't have a crystal ball stand you might like to use a small cushion or a silk handkerchief purchased and reserved specially for this purpose.

Tip

To amplify your crystal ball gazing, you can use a gemstone sphere as a compliment to the crystal ball. Simply having a gemstone sphere resting next the crystal ball can augment your diving two fold.

Sit down and relax. Lay your hands gently on the ball for a minute or two in order to energise it and strengthen your psychic rapport. Whilst holding the crystal ball, think about the purpose of this scrying session. If appropriate try to visualise the subject of your question. Some people like to ask the question out loud, others prefer to internalise it.

Now, remove your hands from the crystal. Look into the crystal, stare deeply. Allow your eyes to relax and become slightly unfocused. After a little while you should see a mist or smoke forming in the crystal. Let this mist grow and fill the ball, then visualise it gradually clearing to reveal images within the crystal.

The images you see might not be what you expected. That's OK, don't fight them. Your subconscious mind knows what information you need. Many people find that when they first begin to use a crystal ball, the images have nothing to do with what they focus on. This is because your mind is not yet adjusted at being able to grasp and focus on the energies being past from your subconscious into the crystal ball itself. Think of the mental energies going from your mind to the crystal ball as a funnel. The base or "tip" of the funnel is your subconscious energies and that energy is being directed upwards towards your conscious mind which is the mid point of the funnel. The conscious part of the mind that receives the subconscious energy then "spills" it into the crystal ball to form those images from the subconscious, which would be the mouth of the funnel.

Since divination uses both the subsconscious and conscious part of the mind at the same time it can be rather difficult to concentrate on both at once. Your subconscious is where the energy is stemming from. It passes it upwards to your conscious which is needed to act on that energy into the crystal ball. Without the conscious mind you would be in more of a deep meditated state and your eyes would not be able to consciously focus or input the images within the crystal ball.

As noted, it is perfectly OK that the first couple times you divine with a crystal ball the images are not related to what it is you want. The fact you are able to see ANYTHING in the crystal ball is showing progress. The more you work with the crystal ball, the better you will get at being able to see exactly what it is you want to see by manipulating your subconscious energies to your conscious energies, and then to the crystal ball. Either way, just let the images flow, changing and taking you wherever they choose to go. Don't try to rationalise now, time for that later.

Step 3. Closing The Crystal Ball Session

Let the images slowly fade back into the crystal ball. Don't just stop the session suddenly, instead reverse the process you used at the beginning.

Visualise the mists coming back and covering the images, then receding to return the ball to its natural state.

Thank your crystal ball and put it away carefully wrapped within a dark cloth is best as dark cloth keeps the energies of the ball contained within it and prevents it from leaking out.

It is also always best to ensure you cleanse your crystal ball. A good, fast, and simple way of doing this is to simply light a sage smudge stick and or sage incense and move the ball around the smoke before you place it back for storage. Another quick and easy way to cleanse your crystal ball would be to give it a dip in salt water for roughly one minute. You do not want to soak it too long in salt as it can damage and ruin the crystal ball.

Basic Steps For Using A Crystal Ball

Celtic Tribes and Druids are of the earliest known peoples to have used crystal balls in divination, as early as 2000 BC. During central Europe's Medieval Period (AD 500-1500), seers, wizards, sorcerers, psychics, gypsies, fortune tellers, and all other types of diviners also used crystals to "see" into the past, present, or future.

Crystal balls have been used as sacred tools by diverse peoples for thousands of years. It is important to remember that crystals are sacred tools and to treat them as such, keeping them on your home altar or other sacred space when they are not in use. It is also advised to keep your crystal ball covered with a black cloth to prevent the light from reaching it when it isn't in use.

Upon obtaining a new crystal ball or any other sacred stones, I like to sleep with it for at least 4 nights to begin establishing a connection. (cleanse it first) During this time your crystal ball will most likely share its name with you. When speaking to your crystal ball make sure to call it by its name. A personal bonding with your crystal ball will happen and therefore you should not let others handle or touch your crystal ball.

You should also provide a special bag or box for your crystal ball to protect it during transportation. Use this special bag or box only for your crystal ball.

Like any other sacred tool, your crystal ball will need to be cleansed on a regular basis. Personally, I use sage or sweetgrass to smudge my crystal ball before and after every use. There are many other recommended methods of cleansing you can discover with a little research.

Using Your Crystal Ball

Cleanse your crystal ball. Using your preferred method always cleanse your crystal prior to every use.

Turn out all artificial light sources, close drapes and darken your room.a background light source such as a lit candle should be used in an otherwise darkened room. A white candle representing purity, or a purple candle representing higher spiritual purpose are good to use. As you progress you can use other colors according to your purpose for the session. Be sure to clearly state that you will only allow positive energies to enter otherwise the door is open for any energy to enter. I like to create a circle to work in by cleansing and protecting the space using sage to smudge the area.

Relax and breathe deeply and rhythmically. Allow all tensions and negativity to flow out of you as you exhale each breath. Ground yourself and as you inhale bring in the energy of the Light, focus your thoughts on your purpose for the session and respectfully ask for the answers to be shown.

When you are completely relaxed, centered and focused, open your eyes and allow your eyes to drift to a spot on your crystal ball that you feel drawn to. Fixate your eyes on that spot and allow your vision to go fuzzy (like when daydreaming) and gaze at that spot actually allowing that daydreaming gaze to move through and past the spot. Simply allow this to happen, don't try to force it. Clear your mind of all thoughts, continue to breathe deeply and rhythmically allowing a state of light meditation. At this time your crystal may begin to appear smoky, cloudy or to darken.

Allow this to happen without breaking your meditation state. If you do lose your meditation state, simply begin again. Remember, practice makes perfect! You may begin to see images, experience feelings, or hear communications. Just go with the flow and don't try to interpret, analyze or make sense of your experience at this time. Just relax and allow it to happen. Also, make sure you aren't trying to create images the way you want to see them. Set aside personal judgments, wants and desires, stop your own thoughts and ideas and be open to what the crystal ball will show you even though it may not be what you want or think it should be.

You may also have physical sensations such as tingling, vibration, heat, or cold. This is normal. The crystal will raise or lower your personal vibration and bring you into the balance and harmony necessary for spiritual connection so that communication can easily happen.

Make note of what you see within your crystal ball. You may find that when in the beginning you have difficulty remembering what you see during your session. Have a note pad and pencil handy and try writing down what you see. A tape recorder works also to record what you see. While writing or speaking to your recorder maintain your meditation state without losing your focus. This will take some practice as speaking or writing will in the beginning have a tendency to bring you out of your trance state. You can enhance your ability to maintain your meditation state during physical activity by learning to do walking meditation. I like to practice walking meditation while out in nature, walking upon a trail through the woods. Use the same technique of deep, rhythmic breathing, releasing tensions, relax, letting your vision go fuzzy and clearing your mind of thoughts

When you have finished your session, allow yourself to return to the physical present. Refocus your eyes and breathe deeply, and ground yourself again in the physical plane. Be aware of your feelings at this time. You may feel your energy shift as you break the connection with your crystal, you may feel rested like you've just awakened from a nap, and you may feel energized. To fully ground yourself have a small snack and drink some water.

Cleanse your crystal ball and return it to its place on your altar or sacred space you have designated for it. Be sure to thank your crystal ball for its help.

Learning to work effectively with your crystal ball will take a lot of practice. Be patient. Don't be discouraged if it doesn't work the first few times. Be persistent, keep working at it and when you finally connect with your crystal ball it will work.

Light Crystal Display - The Clear Future Of Monitors

The use of liquid crystals has been a breakthrough in monitor technology as well as in various display applications such as watches, televisions, and cellular phones among many others. The old CRT Monitors have been huge and bulky while the use of liquid crystals in every pixel has allowed a slim and sleeker look for monitors and display devices. LCD monitors are also electricity efficient, instead of having monitors that consumes a large amount of energy, LCD monitors require minimum energy consumption and it can also be made to run on batteries. That is why it is very versatile and can be used in many different mobile devices.

LCD monitors have a distinctive amount of pixels or fixed-pixel-array displays. In simpler terms, LCD monitors have a native resolution or a specific set of pixel density which in turn displays a specific resolution. The display resolution or pixel dimension tells the customers about the capability of the monitor to clearly display an image. All LCD monitors of the same sizes display the same resolution because all LCD monitors have native resolutions regardless of what brand it is. Putting a different resolution outside the native resolution will cause extrapolation; this causes multiple pixels to produce the same image causing a blurry display. Buyers need to be advised that buying large LCD monitors will actually lead to smaller image displays, this is one of a few cases wherein bigger is actually smaller.

Buying an LCD monitor is definitely a cost effective decision on the buyer's part. The advantages that LCD monitors present far outweighs the very minor special considerations. Compared to cathode ray tube monitors or

CRT's, LCD monitors generate less radiation because there is no build-up of heat on its backside. It is very easy on the eyes and working with it is far less stressful and straining. It does not contain phosphorus and thus it will not cause any image burns during prolonged pauses. Aside from its modern and stylish look, LCD's are very cheap and easy on the budget, it can also help lessen monthly electrical expenses since it consumes less energy during usage and while on stand-by. When buying LCD monitors choose the ones which are suitable for your needs in terms of display resolutions. Though it is quite appealing to have huge widescreen monitors, try to see how it looks when you open websites and documents so that you can check out if they are suitable for your needs. Ask for energy save devices that will add more savings from your bills.

What to Consider When Buying an LCD Monitor a lot of clients drop by and have a barrage of queries about Liquid Crystal Display Monitors. A lot of clients do want to change their computer monitors; however, most of them are still quite hesitant to actually buy them. This is mostly because of the many aspects that you need to consider when buying an LCD monitor. Contrary to popular belief, LCD monitors are not expensive, in fact, it might even cost as much as when you first bought your old CRT monitor. It is also quite the money saver, so you really are getting quite a value for your money. In order to shed some light with regards to the amazing capabilities of LCD Monitors, here is a list of the most frequently asked questions about them and their answers.

What is native resolution?

The screen sizes for monitors are expressed in pixels (e.g., 1024x768). CRT monitors have various numbers of pixels, but LCD monitors however have only a single value or number of pixels no matter what brand they are as long as they have the same sizes. This means that all LCD monitors have a designated resolution that clients should consider because if they want the best results, they will have to comply. Bigger LCD monitors will mean that the images displayed will be much smaller while smaller monitors will actually display bigger images.

What is aspect ratio?

Aspect ratio is the ratio of the number of horizontal pixels to vertical pixels. Most monitors have aspect ratios of 4:3. The new widescreen LCD monitors however, have aspect ratios of up to 16:10, the high definition capabilities of LCD monitors can even have up to 16:9 while ultra wide monitors have a whopping 2:1 aspect ratio. This displays the far more extensive capabilities of an LCD monitor in terms of image clarity and definition.

What is Response time?

In order for the liquid crystals to display a color or an image in a specific area of the monitor, an electric current must pass through the LCD panels. The amount of time that it takes for the current to pass through the panels and the amount of time it takes the liquid crystals to alter it state, to turn on or turn off is called the response time. Response time does not only refer to the turning on or turning off of the monitor but also in displaying bright images as well as dark or black backgrounds. In general, LCD monitors' response time is quite fast. The rising time or the time it takes to turn on is very fast but the falling time or the time it takes to turn off is a little bit slower that is why you will notice a short blur when images suddenly shift to bright streaks on the monitor with a dark background. This is a factor to consider especially when you are buying an LCD monitor for gaming.

What is viewing angle?

As the electric current runs through the LCD panel, the pixel displays the corresponding shade. The pixel however displays the shade directly in front of it towards the viewer seated directly in front of the monitor. This characteristic of the LCD monitor does not allow for clear images when the monitor is viewed on the side or any other angle other than directly in front of the monitor. Though it does require a straight on viewing, this characteristic is actually a sought after feature especially when clients would prefer more privacy with their screen. This is also a great reason why clients often times opt for dual widescreen monitors.

What is Brightness?

Brightness is the capability of the monitor to radiate light or display color. Most of the new monitors have the capability to be very bright. This allows the clients' eyes to be most comfortable during prolonged use. New LCD monitors have advanced features when adjusting brightness. Adjusting the brightness depends on the clients' personal choice. Having a monitor that is very bright can at times be helpful while at time this can also be bad especially when the ambient light is low. New LCD monitors can automatically adjust the brightness of the monitors through sensors and thus it can be quite advantageous to opt for them.

Is image quality important?

Definitely yes, buying LCD monitors is all about getting the best quality images and videos. Having the best images on your monitor together with having the ease that LCD monitors have on the eyes is by far one of the most enticing aspects when buying one. Since CRT monitors are quite limited in their image displays, LCD monitors offer clients precise, crisp and clear images because of its very wide range of aspect ratios and resolutions ranging from widescreens to high definition capabilities that display life like images. The image quality of LCD monitors is definitely one of the main reasons why clients fall in love at first sight for them.

Shopping tips in buying LCD monitors

LCD monitors are clearly the future of computer monitors and other display devices. Its cutting edge advantages and features are clearly what next generation monitors should be. When shopping for monitors, try before you buy. Ask the technician to turn it on for you before you buy it. View the images on the screen and try opening web pages and documents on it that you routinely view or open at home and see if the image display is suitable for your eyes. Check on the brightness of the screen and try out different sizes. Each size displays a different resolution, so make sure that you find one that suits you best. If you need to replace old CRT's then why not go all out and buy the best, try out High Definition monitors and I'm sure you will be amazed at the results. You also need to consider screen real estate. Screen real estate is the amount of space that you can work with on your desktop. Other desktops do display bigger images but provide less screen real estate. You wouldn't want to see applications and pages overcrowding your monitor right? Check screen real estate and see if you have enough space to view pages and applications without having to scroll through documents as if they were a mile long. If you definitely need a lot of space then I suggest you go for dual screens. Dual monitor screens definitely make your desk look cool, it also creates a greater screen space for you to work on comfortably (I personally use a total of four LCD screens in my office). Dual LCD screens are definitely the way to go for all your multi-tasking needs. Look for monitors that have USB ports on the side. Having USB ports can increase efficiency and accessibility. This helps a lot especially when most of the ports are located below your desk in the CPU. You can also try out monitors with built-in Speakers. The speakers can accentuate your existing audio devices and can possible create a sensor round sound atmosphere. In shopping for monitors, always try out the newest models with the most accessories and features.

If clients are interested in getting rid of those hulking CRT's which strain the eyes and generate poor image quality, you can inquire about high quality LCD monitors and come guaranteed to satisfy the client's expectations here at www.etechonline.co.nz. Electrical technology online is a New Zealand based company that sells various electrical gadgets and appliances as well as high performance monitors that are a value for your budget. For a computer monitor come and visit us, take a look at our wide array of LCD monitors as well as many other products. We guarantee that clients will get superior service online and best quality products delivered at the door step.

Natural Crystals And Stones - Their Metaphysical Qualities And Uses

Over the centuries, people from all over the world have been intrigued by the metaphysical qualities of stones, or more appropriately called minerals. It has been recognized that all that exists is in a constant state of vibration, and crystalline structures have a particularly stable vibration which resists the influence of other vibration frequencies.

Minerals, particularly in their crystalline form, stimulate healing based upon the property of sympathetic vibration or resonance. They have very specific points of resonance with one of our seven major energy centers (chakras). The colours of the stones seem to have a bearing on the qualities of the vibrations. This is more or less similar to the colours represented by the seven charkas which also coincide with the seven colours of the rainbow. (Crown chakra - violet, Blow chakra - indigo, Throat chakra-blue, Heart chakra - green, Solar Plexus chakra - yellow), Sacral chakra - orange, and Base chakra red). These resonant frequencies set up an electromagnetic field.

If we believe that all human beings have interweaving energy bodies (human aura) beyond their physical shell, and they are being electromagnetic in nature, it naturally follows that they can be influenced by the electromagnetic resonance of minerals and crystals.

Diseases and illnesses have been attributed to disharmony in thought patterns, causing irregular energy flow within subtle (non-physical), the etheric and physical bodies;

therefore, prolonged exposure to the positive vibration of stones may have a healing effect. Other than their healing effects, minerals also offer protection against negativities and in a way bring good luck to us.

Amulets and Talisman to ward away ghosts.

Certain stones, especially those of celestial origins appear to have the power to drive away unwanted or negative energy. These are stones like those from the meteorite family - tektite, moldavites, iron or nickel meteorites - can actually ward off evil spirits. When carved with images of Buddha or deities, or when they are specifically enchanted by advanced practitioners, they can be used as very powerful talismans or amulets.

So, it is also believed that the wearing of certain amulets or talismans would protect you against ghosts. Also, some also feels that certain stones, especially the quartz family, (White Quartz, Amethyst, Ametrine, Citrine and Smoky Quartz) can offer the same protection. Other protective stones include, diamond, pyrite, hematite, obsidian, black star sapphire, black diopside, and jet. Personally, I understand that stones have a varying degree of electro-magnetic radiation. When they are worn on our body, they serve to strengthen our body energy vibration, sort of casting a protective shield over us.

One very powerful talisman I have is the image of the Earth Store (Dichang) Bodhisattva made of tektite. I also have a bracelet made of pyrite and amber, and I use to have it with me whenever I traveled overseas. In my arsenal, I also have bracelets and pendants made of iron meteorite, and they are also very potent in warding off negativities. It is also believed those moonstones are good protective stones for overseas traveling especially crossing waters. I always keep a few pieces of tumbled moonstones in my luggage.

For those who are frightened of ghosts when traveling overseas and staying in hotel rooms , they can try arranging their shoes in the Ying Yang manner - one with the sole facing up while the other in the normal position - at the foot of their beds.

Amulets and talismans are similarly charged with strong vibrations by their makers - monks and priests alike, and they serve the same purpose as the stones. At my level, I am able to magnetize stones and any objects to confer upon them stronger radiation by using my energisation method or by chanting of mantras.

Spirits In Stones

There are belief that some stones contain memories of the past while some become dwelling place for some life forms, just like the hermit crabs that inhabit the shell after the shellfish have died. My spiritual friend Stella has the ability to communicate with stones and she claimed she often saw impish looking creatures residing in some stones. Once I was meditating with one Labradorite ball (a kind of felspar stone which is opaque with luminous blue against grey background) and spotted images of a woman clad in Greek-like gown amidst some Roman like pillars inside the stone. She had almond shape eyes and shape features and appeared annoyed by my unwelcome intrusion. There was another stone, a piece of Rhodonite - a pink colour stone with black Manganese steaks, that I could see images of dome shapes structure. I also recalled another instance when an old lady handed me a piece of jade which she retrieved from the exhumed grave of her mother died long ago, and asked me whether it was alright for her daughter-in-law to wear it. The moment I picked up the jewelry I could feel a painful sensation in my stomach. I asked her whether she could recall whether her mother suffered some sort of ailment of the stomach, and she confirmed it. I cleansed the stone for her but she told me she had changed her mind about giving it to her daughter-in-law and instead chose to keep it in the jewelry box. Jade is said to have the unusual quality of protecting its owner. It would break into pieces whenever the wearer encounter dangerous situations; the folklore has it that it blocks off the dangers on behalf of its owner.

Stones For Attracting Fortune

Chinese believes that wearing of certain stones would bring them good fortune. Jade is the most favoured stone adorn not only to bring good luck to the wearer but it also offers protection as well. For those gamblers who are ever hopeful windfall, they may wear yellow gemstones - yellow sapphire, topaz, or citrine. Some may even carry a pyrite doughnut together with a dollar coin in their wallet. Green stones are for attracting wealth generated from career, and they include not only jade but also emerald, peridot, quartz with chloride inclusions, aventurine, malachite, and amazonite. Besides wearing them as semi-precious stones set in rings and pendants, some of the tumbled stones (aventurine, malachite, and amazonite) can be placed in cash registers to help enhance daily takings from retailed businesses.

Stones and Feng-shui

Feng-Shui, or Geomancy, is in a manner of speaking also about energy

Energy caused by the landscape, magnetic forces and flows, seasonal fluctuations in energy flows, celestial and planetary influences, and positioning of static objects in the environment, and how your own body energy copes with and resonates with all these causes of energy. The western application of Feng-Shui is to bring an array of scientific equipment into a location and test out the various forms of energy in the area. If you are sensitive to energy, you can actually feel the influence of "Feng-Shui" - the good and bad "Chi" - rather than relying entirely on the Feng Shui principles practiced by the masters. Since stones have positive vibrational energy, they can be deployed to improve the Feng-shui of the building if placed at the correct position.

For example, the left hand corner of the main hall of the house diagonally opposite the entrance is considered the wealth position; to

enhance positive energy in this corner one could emplace amethyst geode. This is a better substitute for putting round leaf plants there, as traditionally recommended by Feng-shui masters. Other than putting up mirrors or wind chimes at our windows to block off negative energy from some ill-formed structures or landscape facing our house, we could hang faceted cut crystal balls. Against the sunlight, these faceted balls could reflect specks of rainbow lights into the house and create a wonderful sight as they are seen as if dancing on the walls.

Gemstones And Their Historic Metaphysical Properties

Crystals have been companions to man in one way or another since the beginning of time. For those of you that recognize the pre-history of Lemuria and Atlantis, it is common knowledge that these peoples were using quartz and other gemstones for energy sources, communications, data storage, and weaponry.

Ancient priestesses painted their faces with white gypsum for purification and to emulate the goddesses of light they served. Most ancient cultures used gems for healing. According to the Bible, the twelve tribes of Israel were each represented by twelve corresponding precious stones. Nobility of all cultures encrusted their palaces and sacred places with precious gems. In Asian cultures, crystals were passed through generations as well as placed during burial with deceased love ones, a practice that still survives today.

In our modern age, the power of crystals cannot be denied. Computers, telecommunications, data storage, memory chips, etc. depend mainly on silicon dioxide, aka - quartz crystal. Rubies and sapphires make laser technology possible, and the building industry depends heavily on minerals such as gypsum, also known as a form of selenite. The military relies on beryllium extracted from such gems as "tiffany stone" for making missiles and warheads, and the drug lithium is still extracted to some degree from quartz with lithium deposits.

On a metaphysical level, crystals are finally beginning to get the mainstream recognition they deserve for supplementing our physical, emotional and spiritual health. I mention them as a supplement since we alone hold the ability to completely heal ourselves at the time of our choosing. Crystals are wonderful tools to assist us in these processes. It is also interesting to note that although we often refer to gemstones as crystals, everything of physical matter in our dimension has a crystalline structure at its simplest form, even man made items such as plastics, so definitely a concept to keep in mind when we consider the idea of "clearing" and "programming" crystals later in this discussion.

Even the precious gemstones that are not as popular in the metaphysical circles have their affinities. For example, diamonds are reputed to draw abundance to their wearer, along with consistency, fidelity, confidence, and purity. Diamonds are one of the gems said to improve physical vision. Emeralds are considered to be quite helpful at facilitating healing in the physical body, and rubies, the stone of nobility, assist in spiritual wisdom, strengthening businesses, imparting good physical health, and knowledge. Garnets are one of the original stones of commitment on all levels, life purpose, relationships, and self (found on many antique engagement rings) thought to strengthen the heart, lungs, and blood. It is worthy to note that these attributes are considered by many metaphysical crystal practitioners to be exactly the same whether a precious gem is natural or man-made.

At a time when many are finally comfortable displaying their cherished crystal specimens to all, it is a good idea to do a little research as to where in the home a gem would be most comfortable and able to impart its gifts. Stones such as selenite, celestite, (geode form), and kyanite (there are certainly others) do not do well in a damp environment and will discolor if not break apart from too much moisture. Amethyst, celestite, and rose quartz may fade if placed in an area with too much UV lighting. A front door can benefit from the display of red tiger's eye, (sometimes called dragons' eye) a manifesting stone that will also chase away negativity. Hallways are thought to benefit from any sparkly or bright colored gems such as sulphur or hematite. Bedrooms can be given a cozy, feminine charm with the addition of rich, dark colored stones, (especially when in spherical or egg forms) such as lapis lazuli, hematite and obsidian, the latter two having grounding affinities. Amethyst placed under the foot (never at the head...too energizing!) of the bed is believed to bring harmony to married relationships, or draw a love to a single person. Moss agate beside the bed is thought to ward off nightmares, amber makes waking in the morning more bearable, and certainly the addition of angelic stones such as celestite or angelite couldn't hurt. These are just a tiny sampling of the possibilities of placing gems within the home.

There are a good number of gemstones making their way onto the scene that perhaps are not as popular, but are truly worth researching. Rhodocrosite, for example, is considered to be the "yang" version of rose quartz. It is often referred to as the stone of compassion in action, a beautiful term for such a lovely gem also attributed to drawing positive soulmates to us, and our inner child out. Rhodocrosite exhibits a broad range of pink colors from opaque with gray undertones to a gel pink in its gem grade forms. Larimar is a recently rediscovered stone (1974?) that brings calm and clarity to its wearer and boasts a striking range of blue-greens and whites reminiscent of Caribbean waves. This is appropriate given that it is only found in the

Dominican Republic, and has long been called "dolphin stone" or Atlantis stone". Larimar is the gem foretold to be discovered at an appropriate time to "Atlantis' rising" by the late Edgar Cayce.

On the subject of the abundance of gems making their way into the world markets at a fast pace, this must be a time when these treasures are ready to surface. Everything certainly happens in divine timing, and although they may have been brought to the surface, they are still happily here on the Earth to assist us and bring us their great beauty. Gemstones such as kyanite which were previously only available as rough pieces for home display or carrying in a pouch are now available in bead and pendant form, a wonderful way to combine healing with fashion.

When choosing a gemstone, it is important to "go with your gut" and let your intuition guide your selection. Make sure the stone "feels right" to you. Consider the things you are trying to draw into or out of your life, and start researching the crystal realm. You will be able to get to the point where you could look at a gemstone on eBay and know it is calling to you. Many believe, and with good reason, that just as all other inhabitants of the natural world are considered to have, that crystals have a resident "Deva" within that gives each gem its unique personality. Some say they can actually hear the little beings singing or talking. Perhaps this is an aspect of what we are drawn to in choosing a stone? Whatever the case, no two gemstones are alike, and everyone will be guided to the best one for their needs.

There is a good bit of discussion on "clearing" crystals, and this is certainly something to consider, even if the only gems you own are on your wedding band or heirloom jewelry. It is believed that gemstones pick up and absorb negative vibrations. Perhaps this is one of the ways in which they help us. I have personally observed some of my clear quartz crystals becoming cloudy over time, then more transparent after i use a technique to clear them. One of the most common, and damaging ways to clear a crystal has been to bury it in sea salt or soak it in salt water. Many still consider this the best way to clear a crystal of unwanted energies, but it is certainly at the expense of the crystal. Salt dehydrates the stones and can make them susceptible to breakage and losing luster, not to mention how this may affect the healing properties of the stone. There are many other ways to clear a crystal that are healthier to them. An additional note on salt is that it is a known absorber of negative energies, so if the salt itself is not cleared, just imagine what could end up in the stone additional. I'll place an asterisk * next to techniques that can also be used to clear salt.

Forming an intention of clearing anything is just as important as the actual clearing, the clearing methods themselves being once again a facilitating factor. One simple way to clear crystals involves the use of sage or incense for smudging*. You simply form the intention in your mind that you are clearing any negative or non-useful energies from your stone as you wave the smoke around it. It is helpful to follow sage smudging with an incense of your choice (frankincense is good) since sage effectively removes so much that the energy needs to be refilled (this comes from a Native American so I trust it). You can also bury the crystal in dried herbs such as rose petals or sage and leave it for a day or so. Burying in the ground or in a flower pot is yet another option but the crystal may get some mud deposits on it. Again, a day or so, trusting your intuition on this, will suffice. Leaving the crystals in full moonlight is considered another effective method of clearing. Sunlight is good*, but it depends on the sunlight and the crystal, since as mentioned earlier, some stones fade in UV light and faults within the gem may cause the piece to crack if the sun is too intense. There are crystals that are considered to never need clearing, and have the ability to clear other gems placed on or near them. Selenite, kyanite, and citrine* are three of these. In fact, a kindly merchant at a gem show showed me a technique of standing in a triangle formed of selenite rods...it was an amazing sensation of clearing on my energetic and physical body! Running a stone under water (no extreme temperatures) is a quick clearing method, and then there is just the old standby of trusting your own power and sending your energetic affirmations through your crystal* to clear it squeaky clean.

If you are using your crystals for healing, remember to also set an intention for each crystal that will act as a program, as crystals, especially quartz, are amazing storehouses for data and energy.

Thank for making it through to the end of *Crystals for Beginners: the Ultimate Beginners Guide to Discover the Secret Power of Crystals and Stones.* Let's hope it was informative and able to provide you with all of the tools you need.

The next step is to put the techniques and questions you read about into action.

Finally, if you found this book useful in any way, a review on Amazon is always appreciated!

Printed in Great
Britain
by Amazon